WALTHAM FOREST LIBRARIES

904 000 00429374

Waltham Forest Libraries	
904 000 00429374	
Askews & Holts	05-Jun-2015
641.692 OLP	£12.99
4674562	

COOKING WITH
TINNED
FISH

PAVILION

CONTENTS

INTRODUCTION

Travelling to fishing communities all over the world inspired me to give the fishermen and their wonderful stories their place on the cookbook shelves. Their sustainably caught fish is the foundation of the recipes in this book. By supporting sustainable fish, we give endangered fish populations the opportunity to recover. So let's get to work with sustainable fish: the fisherman with his nets and rods, the cook with pots and pans.

To make sure the fish lover is able to enjoy both preserved and fresh fish in the future, many fisheries will have to start operating differently from how they are now. And by buying only sustainable and fresh fish, the consumer can make an important contribution to that endeavour.

If there's one thing I've learned during my travels, it's the fact we can make a big impact on sustainability by making ethical choices over tinned fish. After all, a lot of wild fish ends up in a tin. These fish are accessible and affordable to many, even if you're on a budget, and with tinned fish you can easily prepare tasty and nutritious meals.

We often don't know where fish comes from and how it was caught. The lack of good information prevents consumers from making the right choices to suit their lifestyle. Because they have labels, it is easy for the manufacturer to inform the consumer about what fish are in the tin, how they were caught and what happened to them between the sea and the tin. Transparency makes all the difference. You need to know the stories behind the product in order to love the product. That's why in this book you won't just find unexpected recipes, you'll also get to know the fishermen and manufacturers. They made the conscious decision to fish with the environment in mind or use sustainable fish in their produce. By opting for sustainable produce, the consumer can in turn influence fishing methods and fish populations.

MORE and more tinned fish manufacturers are taking responsibility by adding certification labels from organisations such as the MSC, the Marine Stewardship Council. The MSC continually verify fisheries' compliance with protocols; for example, minimising the bycatch of dolphins caught in tuna nets. The certification label assures the consumer that the fish they've bought has come from fisheries operating under sustainable fishing guidelines.

IN addition to the fishing method, flavour is of course very important in the produce. Mass production and anonymity often impact negatively on flavour and quality. I've found that doesn't have to be the case. That's why I founded Fish Tales, offering the tastiest tinned fish, smoked or fresh, caught by environmentally responsible fishermen. They view the seas and oceans as the source of all life. Their fish has no artificial flavour. Try it, taste the difference and judge for yourself.

TINNED fish is surprisingly versatile in the kitchen. We took the task of creating sumptuous dishes with tinned fish as a challenge. The results may surprise you. We selected 50 of the best recipes from an impressive collection. This book offers you the best of both worlds: fresh produce combined with tinned tuna, salmon, crab, cockles, mackerel, mussels, anchovies and sardines.

BART VAN OLPHEN, AUGUST 2014

LOOKING BACK

THE life of our tinned fish starts, oddly enough, with glass. At the end of the eighteenth century the industrial revolution led to a sharp rise in the population of the industrialised nations; and more people called for more food. Fridges hadn't been invented yet and transportation of fresh produce was slow. Preserving methods such as drying, smoking, pickling, curing and conserving in fat or sugar offered little relief and were too expensive on a large scale. Cheaply and safely preserved food was supposed to be the solution for the growing need for food. Even Napoleon Bonaparte faced the troubles of perishable foods, which threatened his ambitions. Hungry soldiers are hardly the ideal force to help you win battles, and in 1795 the French government offered a money prize to whoever could make preserved, nutritious food for a soldier's ration.

AT the time, French confectioner Nicolas Appert was experimenting with food. Appert had years of experience in the techniques of making syrups and confectionery, and he began heating jars of food in water up to 100°C/200°F, then cooling them down. Once he had perfected the technique, he achieved the desired outcome: he was able to successfully preserve meat, vegetables and fruit by the technique now known as sterilisation. Although preserving fruit by heating it is a technique that had been around long before Appert, he was the first to research the effects of airtight seals and applying high temperatures to food. Appert eventually supplied the navy, which intended to use his preserved fruit to prevent their crew from contracting scurvy. When his efforts proved successful, the navy informed the French government who awarded Appert the prize money in 1810. Appert's jars enabled the troops to charge into battle well fed, and his conserving method survived Napoleon Bonaparte. The confectioner could easily be seen as a food scientist *avant la lettre* and the founder of convenience food. Louis Pasteur would later improve on Appert's technique, turning down the heat by about thirty degrees. Pasteurisation killed enough harmful bacteria and retained more flavour.

THE French government insisted Nicolas Appert should publish his research. *L'Art de conserver, pendant plusieurs années, toutes les substances animals et végétables* is probably one of the first books on preserving food that found its way into many households around the world. In Britain, the book found its way to Pierre Durand, a Frenchman who anglicised his name to Peter Durand. He held a patent for conserving food in glass and tin cans. Appert nudged Durand in the right direction, but Durand didn't pursue the business further and sold his patent cheaply to Donkin, Hall and Gamble. Bryan Donkin recognised the potential of conserving food in tin cans. Tins were lighter than glass, didn't break and were easier to manufacture. Again the navy, this time the Britsh navy, served as the testing ground. The rest is history: the British tin came, saw and conquered. The French have one more addition to the history of tinned food. Grimod de la Reynière, a friend of Nicolas Appert, wrote about the sardines of Nantes conserved in butter, oil and vinegar, before Donkin went full steam ahead with his tins. The efforts of Nicolas Appert and later Louis Pasteur form the basis of the food industry as we now know it. Even now the availability of affordable conserved food means not having to go hungry for millions of people around the world.

FROM TINSMITH TO AUTOCLAVE

ONCE upon a time tins were super sexy. The only tins getting any respect these days are the tin cans on wheels. Once it became available, preservation techniques such as freezing rapidly overtook the tin. However, it's time the tin gets some more recognition. The modern tin is strong, hygienic and easily recyclable. The use of corrosion-resistant, light aluminium and thinner metal increase the recycling options and lower the carbon footprint in production and transport. The materials are pliable and easy to open: great for whether you are in the kitchen or trekking through the Andes. The tins' contents are portioned so there is less waste. Most people use the contents in one go, but if you do have any left over, you can remove it from the tin and keep it in a covered container in the fridge a couple of days or even freeze it. Tins always offer a readily available stash of nutritious and reliable food.

IT wasn't always like that. Making tins used to be manual craft. For many, tinsmith was a highly regarded profession. Tinsmiths made all sorts of items by hand from tinplated sheet iron – such as biscuit and cocoa tins. To increase production, the manufacture of tins for foods containing liquids was mechanised. It didn't all work perfectly from the start: the moisture and acid-rich foods caused rust in the tins. The manufacturers were also not able to mechanically seal the tins and opted for bendable, poisonous lead to solder the tins shut. In turn, this made them difficult to open – a chisel was often the opener of choice! However, through trial and error manufacturers kept improving tin cans. The arrival of the tin opener also increased their popularity, although the first tin opener wasn't exactly fit for domestic use. It was basically a modified bayonet that made it easier for soldiers to get to their baked beans. Thinner metal made way for the more useful tool with a cutting wheel.

GALVANISATION with zinc countered rust corrosion, and creasing and welding techniques made lead unnecessary. The acidity continued to be a challenge and for a long time, the metals continued to leave a distinct tin flavour in the food. Eventually the invention of a plastic coating made this a problem of the past.

THE pressure cooker, a seventeenth-century invention by the Frenchman Denis Papin, made it truly possibly to deliver tinned food safely, as high-pressure steam cooked the food more quickly. Two hundred years later, the Brit Charles Chamberlain invented the autoclave, a further development of Papin's pan. The autoclave is used to sterilise food under high pressure and at temperatures reaching 100°C/200°F and higher, doing away with the need for preservatives. Most manufacturers add at least some salt, so they can sterilise more quickly or at lower temperatures. The once infamous, gas-bloated tin of rotten foods is now – even past the expiration date – a thing of the past. Only less stable ingredients like crab are still assisted by stabilising agents in the tin.

THE SEASON IN A TIN

'Tin the fish on the day of catch before sunset.' That's a saying popular with many tinned food manufacturers. They prefer to process fresh goods in season, and for fish this means tinning as soon as possible after catching. Tests have proven that the nutritional value of modern tinned food comes close to that of fresh produce. Storing produce also costs money. By reducing the heating-process time, it also reduces the energy bill. Tinning doesn't guarantee good flavour though; flavour depends on the production methods and the quality of the original produce used. Like all other foods, tinned fish is all about picking the right producers.

This might come as a surprise to many, but tinned fish is a very seasonal product. Not only that but it also comes from well-managed and healthy stocks. The fisheries catch the fish only when the fish is in the right shape for consumption and none of the fish is lost in production. All these aspects are important in maintaining both the quality of the product, the protection of the environment and the sustainability of the fish stocks.

The better producers will provide clear information on the contents of the tin and where it's from. Tinned fish is available from large-scale companies who use multiple canneries that tin other foods in addition to fish. On the other end of the spectrum are many smaller, often family-run, businesses, especially in areas of Europe such as Brittany, the Spanish Basque Country, northern Portugal, Denmark and northern Germany. They tin fish from day catches and use high-quality oil or carefully selected sauces. These products are found in the aisles under their own names or as part of, for example, the Fish Tales range. It is definitely worth reading the label first before making a decision on which tinned fish to buy.

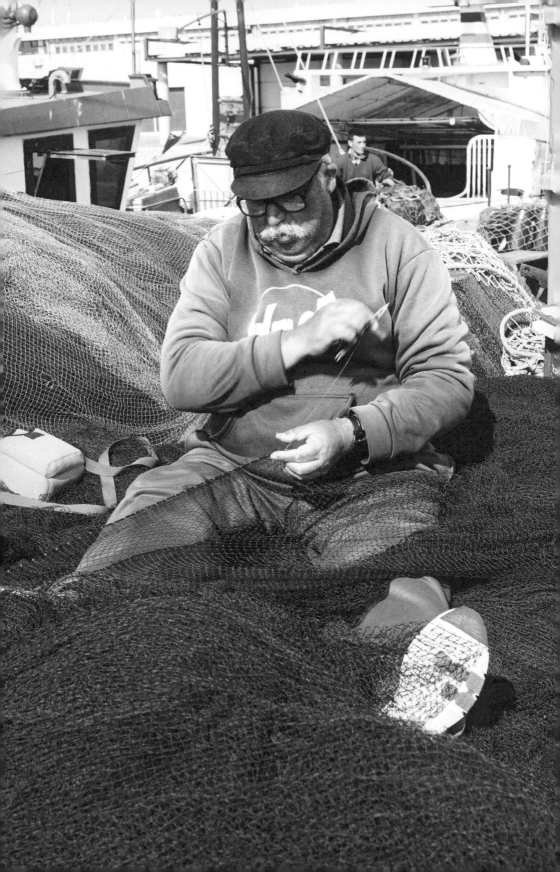

A TALE ABOUT PORTUGUESE FISHING COMMUNITIES

THE fishing village Mastosinhos in Porto once housed more than two hundred *fábricas de conservas*, which mainly processed Portugal's famous sardines. New food safety regulations and a demand for higher quality meant the end for many of these factories. Because they held onto their traditional ways for too long, they weren't able to modernise. A bit further north in the fishing village Póvoa de Varzim, fishing workplaces met their demise. The factories were only running when sardines populated the Portuguese coast – from April to October – but employees would continue to be paid throughout the rest of the year. These businesses valued their employees highly because they would be nowhere without the women – who comprised the bulk of the workforce – who carried out the manual labour. This model, however, was not profitable enough to sustain.

THE family running A Poveira realised they needed a change of approach. They were selling their sardines under the well-known name Minerva and were able to find investors who believed in the future of supplying high-quality tinned fish. Changing their methods would lead to an even higher quality. They closed down their old factories and opened a new cannery in Póvoa de Varzim, where, in addition to sardines, they are able to process different fish, which means employees can work throughout the year.

A Poveira's ultra-modern factory might look less appealing than an old-fashioned version, but its production of the highest-quality tinned fish is what matters. Skilled women are still at the heart of the company. Rather than going into mass production, which often leads to loss of flavour in the final product, A Poveira combines modern techniques with the skilled work of dedicated craftswomen to achieve even better-tasting fish.

MANY manufacturers fill their tins with raw fish which are then heated to 100°C/200°F after sealing – cooking and sterilising the fish at the same time. This approach generally leads to loss of flavour. A Poveira first steam their sardines and mackerel, after which skilled labourers carefully clean and pack the fish into the tins, sometimes with herbs and spices. The tins are then filled with good-quality olive oil, water or a sauce, depending on the product. Finally, the tins are sealed mechanically and briefly sterilised.

A Poveira uses tastings to convince their visitors that their approach works. Premium brand Minerva's Portuguese sardines have a distinctly pure flavour. The Fish Tales sardines are made by the same people. The flesh on the removed bone still has that characteristic rose-tinted colour of fresh sardines. The mackerel's strong flavour and meaty bite also impress.

A WOMEN'S STRONGHOLD

'*Tu é eu, nós dois*', is tattooed on many a woman's skin. You and me, always together. The man at sea, the woman on land, always connected. The men run the seas, but women rule the dockside. They take the crates of fish from the men, sort the fish and clean them in the factories. Men have earned their place in the fish trade though. You can recognise their warehouses by the pictures of famous football teams like FC Porto and Sporting Portugal.

DESIGNER TINNED FISH

A Poveira couldn't have timed the new development better. High-quality tinned fish is gaining in popularity – and not just in Portugal. Young entrepreneurs like José Ricardo Silva are capitalising on this trend.

Silva opened a pop-up store in Porto around Christmas 2013. It was a success and Silva decided to open a permanent shop: Central Conserveira da Invicta. The sardines are supplied by A Poveira and Silva designs the tins himself. You won't find tins as colourful and vibrant as these anywhere else. The Porto town centre is home to a couple of speciality stores, like A Favorita do Bolhão, that stock a wide range of tins.

And here's some more tips to remember when you're on holiday visiting the wonderful city of Lisbon. Go to the Conserveira de Lisboa in the old city centre of Lisbon. You'll find a shop with a 1930s-style interior design where the walls are lined with tins. The proprietors produce their own tinned fish and create sauces to accompany the sardines. Café Sol e Pesca in Lisbon simply has tinned fish with bread and a delightful wine on the menu – a perfect combination. Mercearia das Flores in Porto also serves tinned fish, with the local bread delicacy, broa, made from cornflour. If you want to go upmarket, visit Can the Can in Lisbon where the chef offers innovative dishes using fresh as well as tinned fish.

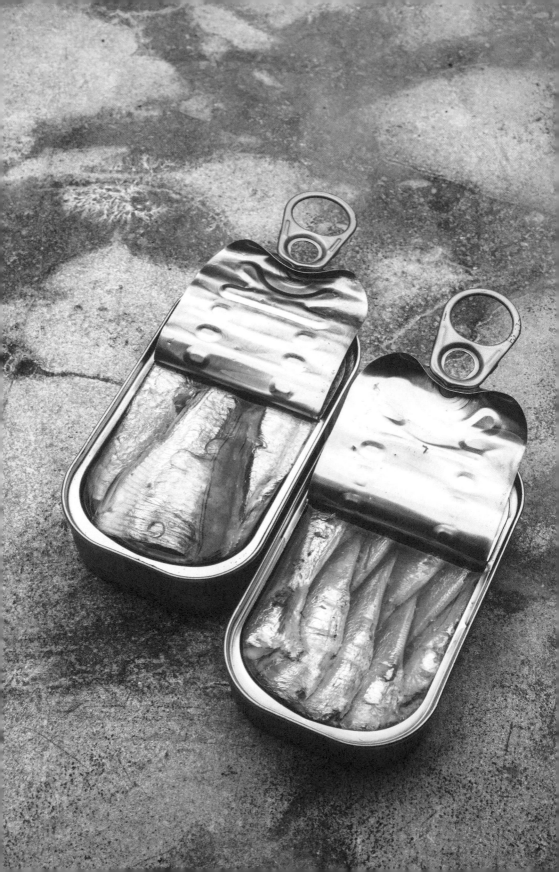

COOKING WITH TINNED FISH

THIS book offers the best of two worlds by combining tinned fish with fresh produce. Tinned fish is very versatile, especially when you're aware of this rule of thumb: fish in water is best used in cold dishes and fish in oil can be used in both hot and cold dishes. This is because fish in water is drier than fish in oil and heat will further dry the fish. Lean fish, like tuna in water, go well with fatty products like mayonnaise and cheese. However, don't be restricted by these rules. If you let your imagination run wild, you'll doubtless create delicious recipes of your own, especially if you use seasonings like lemon, tomato and black and white pepper, which can really lift tinned fish.

THE quality of the oil used with tinned fish can vary wildly. If you've got a good product and the oil smells and tastes good, you can use that oil from the tin in your dishes. If not, just drain the oil and use your own.

COCKLES, crab and mussels are well suited for use in both cold and warm dishes. Remember to add them to a dish like a soup or pasta just before serving only to heat through, otherwise the shellfish can overcook and lose their flavour.

SPECIES	Albacore tuna and skipjack tuna
BINOMIAL NAME	*Thunnus alalunga* and *Katsuwonus pelamis*
FISHING METHODS	Pole and line-caught
MSC CERTIFIED	Predominantly the skipjack fishery in the Maldives, also the American Albacore Fishing Association (AAFA) in the United States and (for more information on the MSC see page 152)
TINNED OPTIONS	Tuna in water, tuna in sunflower oil and tuna in olive oil

WHEN WE CO-EXIST WITH NATURE, THE CATCH WILL BE BOUNTIFUL.

TUNA

IF you want tuna, buy a tin of skipjack, the striped tuna. The skipjack is less threatened in its territories and dolphins don't populate the same areas. The albacore, the white tuna, known in Spain as *bonito del norte*, can also be a sensible choice, provided it is supplied by a fishery known to use sustainable sources.

THE other species of tuna are in worse shape. Most supermarkets now reject tins of yellowfin tuna, and the survival of the famous Atlantic bluefin is seriously threatened, so it is best left alone. Certainly in Western countries, you are increasingly likely only to find skipjack or albacore on the shelves, as more and more supermarkets exclude other types of tuna. If the tin shows the blue MSC eco-label, you know you have certified sustainable fish in your hand.

WHAT is in the tin? Precooked tuna. Albacore is lighter in colour and flavour compared to skipjack. The belly, the expensive and fatty *ventresca*, is mostly sold in flat tins and jars. The other parts of the tuna, including the trimmings, are all packaged in round tins. Whether you use larger or smaller chunks is up to you, but a large chunk of tuna, from a steak, represents the highest quality. Of lower quality is a tin with large chunks pressed together, while the lowest-quality tinned fish consists of many smaller pieces. The quality can vary from good to rather mediocre, but fortunately an increasing number of manufacturers now indicate whether their tin contains steak or chunks, which gives you some options. Finding good tuna is a matter of trying multiple tins by different brands.

THE tastiest and best-quality skipjack is found in the Indian Ocean, near the Maldives, the string of 26 atolls and 1,200 islands with their countless stunning sandy beaches. Tourism is a good source of income for the locals, but the real sharks among them choose a life on the seas. They can always fall back on peddling drinks and snacks. Week after week, Ali Mohamed and his band of fishermen cast their rods into the ocean. This line-catching method almost completely eliminates the bycatch of vulnerable sea creatures. Tuna live in large schools, which makes rod fishing economically viable. At night, Ali shines his floodlights, attracting small fish like moths to a flame. The fish are pulled aboard and stored in salt-water tanks. The next day they serve as live bait for the tuna.

ALI AND JACK'S GRACEFUL, CONTROLLED LINE FISHING

THE fishermen aren't fazed by the swell of the ocean. They continue to cast their lines relentlessly, as if their lives depended on it. A mist of spray shrouds the ship, which distracts the tuna and they can't see the ship. One by one, the fishermen haul tuna onto the ship until they run out of bait, then they pack up for the day, even if there's plenty of tuna left in the sea. Overfishing is beneficial neither to the fish nor to the fishermen. It is now time to go back to Mandhoo, the fishing village on Laamu Atoll, and rest on the pearly white sand of the coconut palm-shaded Mandhoo Beach.

LINE fishing appears to be the obvious method of countering overfishing, as fishing with nets ensures the catch of large numbers of fish in one go. However, in reality it is less straightforward. Line fishing of endangered fish stocks can be just as harmful to a species. 'Only when we co-exist with nature will the catch be bountiful,' says Ali Mohamed. A truly sustainable fishery relates to more than just the fishing method. Especially in areas where the local population has few alternative means of making a living, fisheries can contribute to supporting local communities. The fishermen in the Maldives are a

good example of this. In the company Horizon, they control the supply chain, from the catch to the tin. Everyone involved in the fishery earns a decent income as an independent entrepreneur. This approach attracts interested buyers who, together with the International Pole and Line Foundation, financially support local initiatives like the fishers school. When you buy MSC-certified tuna, you can rest assured you're supporting environmentally responsible fisheries. However, do note that only 8 per cent of the world's tuna catch complies with these conditions.

On the other side of the planet, on the West Coast of America, tuna fishermen do their bit as well. They have renounced the infamous drift nets, and Jack Webster and his colleagues angle with rod and line for albacore, the white tuna, on the south coast of California. Timing is of the essence when fishing for albacore. When the hook hits the water, the tuna swim towards the hook at 40–50km/25–30mls an hour. The tuna bites and will dive back down immediately. At the precise moment the fish bites, the angler has to forcefully pull the fish out of the water. If the fisherman is just a split second too late, the tuna will drag the rod down into the sea. This approach results in healthy tuna stocks and has the added advantage that dolphins will rarely be tempted to bite baited hooks. As soon as the fish is caught, it is placed in brine at -14°C/7°F. This cooling technique ensures the quality of the fish meat is maintained. When you see the boats in the harbour filled with tuna, it's hard to believe each fish was caught individually. In 2008, this 'One man, one hook, one fish' attitude resulted in an MSC certification for the world's first sustainable tuna fishery.

TUNA SPAGHETTI WITH CAPERS AND OLIVES

olive oil
2 tsp tomato purée
2 red peppers, deseeded and
    diced
3 tins of tuna in olive oil,
    (100g/3½oz drained
    weight per tin), drained
    and flaked
350ml/12fl oz/1½ cups passata

2 tsp capers, rinsed
4 tbsp chopped black olives
1 bay leaf
500g/1lb 2oz spaghetti
100g/3½oz Parmesan cheese,
    freshly shaved
salt and freshly ground black
    pepper

- Heat a dash of olive oil in a large frying pan. Add the tomato purée and fry over a medium heat for 1 minute.
- Add the peppers and fry until al dente.
- Add the tuna and stir to blend the ingredients.
- Add the passata, capers, olives and bay leaf and stir, then leave the sauce to heat through on a low heat, stirring occasionally.
- Meanwhile, bring a pan of water to the boil with a pinch of salt.
- Add the spaghetti and cook until al dente according to the instructions on the packet.
- Drain the spaghetti, then spoon it into serving bowls.
- Turn the heat up under the sauce, stir well and season to taste with black pepper. Spoon on top of the spaghetti.
- Serve with Parmesan cheese in a separate bowl.

CHUNKY TUNA MESS

SNACK/STARTER
SERVES 4

THIS recipe is an adaptation of a traditional Flemish tuna salad called *smos-tuna* – and *smos* means to mess or fiddle with, so this title seemed appropriate for this tasty little salad, which has no measurements. Just mess around with it however you like, as long as you flake the tuna in large chunks.

mayonnaise
crème fraîche
3 tins of tuna in water
(100g/3½oz drained
weight per tin), drained
and flaked into large pieces
1 carrot, grated

1 jar of pickled onions
1 jar of gherkins in vinegar,
cut into chunks
slices of bread, toasted
box of cress
salt and freshly ground black
pepper

- Combine equal quantities of mayonnaise and crème fraîche and season with salt and pepper.
- Mix in chunks of tuna, the grated carrot, pickled onions and gherkins to taste.
- Spoon onto the toast and garnish generously with cress.

VEAL MEDALLION AND TUNA PASTE SANDWICH

SNACK/STARTER
SERVES 4

200ml/7fl oz/generous ¾ cup chicken stock

4 veal medallions, 1cm/½in thick

2 tins of tuna in water (100g/3½oz drained weight per tin), drained

2 eggs, hard-boiled

2 anchovies

3 tbsp mayonnaise

1 tbsp olive oil

1 tsp lemon juice

135g/4¾oz bag of rocket

1 baguette, cut into 4 pieces

2 ripe vine tomatoes, sliced

1 handful of capers

freshly ground white pepper

1 bunch of radishes, washed

- Bring the stock to the boil.
- Add the veal medallions and simmer in the stock for 4 minutes. The meat should still be pink.
- Remove the veal from the stock. You can use the stock as the base for a tasty soup.
- To make the tuna paste, use a food processor or blender to blend 2 tablespoons of the stock with the tuna, eggs, anchovies, mayonnaise, olive oil and lemon juice until completely smooth.
- Divide the rocket among the 4 baguettes. Place the veal medallions on the rocket. Generously spread tuna paste on the medallions.
- Garnish with slices of tomato and sprinkle with capers, then finish with a crack of white pepper.
- Serve the baguettes with the radishes.

TUNA AND TOMATO PASTE MILLE-FEUILLE

SNACK/STARTER
SERVES 4

2 tins of tuna in water
  (100g/3½oz drained
  weight per tin), drained
  and flaked
3 tbsp mayonnaise
2 tbsp crème fraîche
4 sundried tomatoes, drained
  (if from a jar) and
  finely sliced

6 sprigs of rosemary, finely
  chopped
250g/9oz pack of rye
  crispbread
1 red onion, thinly sliced
4 vine tomatoes, sliced
salt and freshly ground white
  pepper

- Using a stick blender, mix together the tuna, mayonnaise, crème fraîche and sundried tomatoes.
- Season with rosemary, salt and pepper.
- Spread the paste on the crispbreads.
- Place the sliced red onion and tomato slices on the tuna paste.
- Layer the crispbreads to make the mille-feuille.

TUNA AIOLI, BACON AND AVOCADO PITTA

SNACK/STARTER
SERVES 4

olive oil
250g/9oz cherry tomatoes,
    halved
100g/3½oz bacon
4 pitta breads
2 ripe avocados
1 lemon
6 garlic cloves
4 slices of bread, crusts removed,
    then toasted

8 tbsp mayonnaise
2 tins of tuna in water
    (100g/3½oz drained
    weight per tin), drained
1 spring onion, chopped
coarse sea salt and freshly
    ground white and black
    pepper

- Heat a dash of oil and fry the tomatoes over a medium-high heat for a couple of minutes.
- Remove from the pan, sprinkle with salt and white pepper and set aside.
- Heat a frying pan and fry the bacon until crispy. Leave to drain on kitchen paper.
- Lightly toast the pitta bread in a toaster or under the grill, then split in half horizontally.
- Halve the avocados and remove the stones. Scoop out the flesh with a spoon, cut into slices and drizzle with lemon juice.
- Using a pestle and mortar, crush the garlic cloves, sea salt, white pepper, 1 tbsp olive oil and a piece of toasted bread. Fold in the mayonnaise.
- Purée the tuna in a food processor or with a stick blender.
- Mix the garlic mayonnaise with the tuna.
- Spread the tuna aioli on the inside of one half of the pittas, then top with the bacon, tomato and avocado. Sprinkle with spring onions and finish with some freshly ground black pepper. Top with the other half of the pitta breads.

TACOS WITH FRESH TUNA SALAD

MAIN COURSE
SERVES 4

4 tbsp mayonnaise
2 tbsp full-fat yogurt
1 tbsp tomato ketchup
2 tbsp olive oil
1 red onion, thinly sliced
3 small gherkins in vinegar,
    drained and finely chopped
1 tbsp capers
2 tbsp lemon juice

1 tbsp freshly ground black
    pepper
3 tins of tuna in water
    (100g/3½oz drained
    weight per tin), drained
    and flaked
4 taco shells
150g/5½oz bag of mixed salad

- Preheat the oven to 190°C/375°F/gas 5.
- Mix together the mayonnaise, yogurt, ketchup and olive oil thoroughly.
- Add the onion, gherkins, capers, lemon juice and black pepper and stir them together well.
- Mix the tuna flakes into the dressing.
- Heat the tacos in the oven for 3 minutes.
- Let the tacos cool a bit, fill with the tuna and serve with the mixed salad.

TUNA PASTE AND ROASTED PEPPER WRAP

STARTER
SERVES 4

2 red peppers, halved and
  deseeded
2 tins of tuna in water
  (100g/3½oz drained
  weight per tin), drained
  and flaked
8 tbsp mild chilli relish
3 tbsp mayonnaise
1 tbsp olive oil

4 tsp chopped thyme leaves
4 small wraps
2 red onions, thinly sliced into
  rings
2 tbsp capers, drained and
  rinsed
salt and freshly ground black
  pepper

- Preheat the grill. Put the peppers on the grill, skin-side up, and grill until the skin blisters and turns black.
- Put the peppers in a plastic container or bag, seal and leave to cool.
- Once cooled, the skin will come loose. Remove the skin and cut the flesh into thin strips. Set aside.
- Preheat the oven to 180°C/350°F/gas 4.
- Using a food processor or stick blender, blend together the tuna, chilli relish, mayonnaise, olive oil, 2 tsp of thyme leaves, salt and pepper.
- Place the wraps in the oven for a few minutes until lightly coloured.
- Spread the tuna paste on the wraps and top with the sliced onions, peppers and capers. Sprinkle over the remaining thyme leaves and some extra pepper. Roll up and enjoy.

WHITE TUNA AND GREEN HERB COUSCOUS SALAD

STARTER
SERVES 4

250g/9oz/scant 1½ cups couscous
chicken stock
olive oil
1 large red or green pepper,
    deseeded and cut into strips
3 tins of tuna in water
    (100g/3½oz drained weight
    per tin), drained and flaked

1 large red onion, cut into rings
a few sprigs of dill
a few sprigs of basil
a few sprigs of flat-leaf parsley
a few chives, cut into long pieces
coarse sea salt and freshly ground
    white pepper

- Cook the couscous in the chicken stock according to the package directions, then leave to cool. Stir with a fork to loosen the grains, then drizzle with olive oil, salt and pepper to taste. Stir again.
- Put the pepper pieces onto four plates or bowls and spoon the couscous over the top. Add the tuna flakes.
- Garnish with the red onion, dill, basil, parsley and chives.
- Drizzle some olive oil over the salad to finish.

SPECIES	Anchovy
BINOMIAL NAME	*Engraulis anchoita*
FISHING METHODS	Pelagic trawling
MSC CERTIFIED	Argentine Anchovy Fishery (Mar del Plata) (for more information on the MSC see page 152)
TINNED OPTIONS	Fillets in oil

SOAKING ANCHOVY IN MILK, WINE OR WATER GREATLY ENHANCES THE CULINARY POSSIBILITIES OF THE HUMBLE FISH.

ANCHOVIES

ANCHOVIES are related to herrings, so they belong to the family of oily fish. Oily fish are perfect for fermenting in brine, which tenderises the meat, and anchovy is no exception, but it is time-consuming. Tinning anchovy in salt and oil is a much quicker technique, but it won't tenderise the fish – in fact it toughens it slightly. Tinned anchovy is not sterilised, because applied heat will only result in fish pulp. The quality of the products can differ, but at least a tin of anchovy is not expensive. Buy a couple and see if you agree: tinned anchovy can surprise you.

THE preserving method limits the capabilities of the tinned anchovy in the kitchen. They are mostly used to add a kick of flavour to dishes. Soaking anchovy in milk, wine or water greatly enhances the culinary possibilities of the humble fish. You can also mellow the saltiness with some butter. Oil offers the adventurous cook the chance to add surprising touches as well, following in the footsteps of the ancient Romans who used the fish sauce *garum* to spice up their dishes. Fish sauce is still widely used in Asian cuisine. In Thai it's called *nam pla*, in Vietnamese *nuoc nam* and in Chinese *yu lu*. All of them use anchovy as the main ingredient. South-European countries like Italy also make their own, very expensive fish sauce from anchovy: *colatura*.

THE ARGENTINES GET IT COMPLETELY

FORTY years ago, Mariano's family's fishery used to fish around Argentina's large seaside resort of Mar del Plata with a fleet of small boats. It was hard making a living that way so the family decided to sell off their boats and invested in a couple of larger vessels. This enabled them to sail further out to sea and fish for anchovy. During that time, Mariano experienced the consequences of overfishing. Something had to change. Mariano chose restrained fishing and had the MSC scrutinise his methods. He got the go-ahead: his is the world's first MSC-certified anchovy fishery. One hopes this milestone will inspire the numerous fisheries along the South American coast, because Latin American fisheries play a big part in the global fish trade. Their approach can make all the difference.

TRUE fish lovers leave tinned fish like anchovy and sardines to mature in order to reach a more complex flavour. Turning the cans keeps the fish from drying out. To accommodate the fish lover, some French producers state the season the fish was caught. The area the anchovy was caught, the name of the boat and the name of the fisherman can also be available: useful information for the consumer who wants to know what they're buying.

ONLY a few manufacturers offer MSC-certified anchovy from Argentine waters. Others would rather not spend the money or, more often, don't see a profit in fish with the blue eco-label. However, they will guarantee the anchovy is caught with ring nets, which eliminates most bycatch. That sounds good, but only the MSC eco-label gives the consumer traceable certainty regarding the fishing method.

RIB EYE STEAK WITH ANCHOVY BUTTER

MAIN COURSE
SERVES 4

2 garlic bulbs, separated and
    peeled
2 tins of anchovy fillets in olive
    oil (50g/1¾oz per tin),
    drained
100g/1¾oz butter

1 shallot, finely chopped
1 lemon
4 x 200g/7oz rib eye steak,
    at room temperature
salt and freshly ground black
    pepper

- Preheat the oven to 200°C/400°F/gas 6.
- Wrap the garlic cloves in kitchen foil and place in the oven.
- After 20 minutes, check on the garlic by squeezing one of the cloves. If it's completely soft, take the parcel out of the oven.
- Using a fork, mash the anchovies into the butter.
- Mix the shallot with a squeeze of lemon juice into the anchovy butter, cover and set aside.
- Trim any excess fat off the meat and cut the fat into cubes.
- Heat a frying pan and fry the cubes over a medium heat until golden brown. Remove from the pan and set aside.
- Season the meat with salt and pepper.
- Fry the meat for a few minutes on each side over a high heat until browned and cooked to your liking. Remove the meat from the pan, cover and leave to rest for at least 5 minutes before slicing.
- Serve the steak with the anchovy butter, the roasted garlic and the fried cubes with an extra sprinkling of black pepper.

CITRUS ANCHOVIES AND GRILLED COURGETTE

STARTER
SERVES 4

juice of 1 lemon, strained
juice of 1 orange, strained
200ml/7fl oz/generous ¾ cup
   balsamic vinegar
a few basil stalks
50g/1¾oz/heaped ⅓ cup pine
   nuts

1 tin of anchovy fillets in olive
   oil (50g/1¾oz), drained
milk (to desalt the anchovy)
groundnut oil
1 courgette
a little olive oil
a few sprigs of thyme

- Put the lemon and orange juice, balsamic vinegar and basil stalks in a pan and boil until reduced by one-third.
- Remove from the heat, take out the stalks and leave to cool, then chill in the fridge.
- Heat a frying pan and toast the pine nuts until golden brown.
- Desalt the anchovies by soaking in lukewarm water or milk for a few minutes, if you like. Drain and pat dry.
- Remove the vinegar from the fridge and beat in a few drops of nut oil.
- Cut the courgette into 3 pieces, then cut the pieces lengthways into slices about 2mm thick. Brush with olive oil and grill on both sides until browned.
- Place the grilled courgette slices on a large plate. Sprinkle the balsamic dressing over the vegetables and serve with the anchovies, pine nuts and thyme leaves.

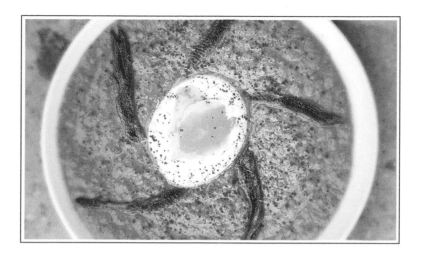

COLD SPANISH SOUP WITH ANCHOVIES

STARTER
SERVES 4

15 ripe vine tomatoes, chopped
a few pieces of stale baguette
6 eggs
6 garlic cloves, peeled
olive oil

cayenne pepper
red wine vinegar
butter
16–20 anchovy fillets
salt

- Using a stick blender, purée the tomatoes, bread, 2 eggs and the garlic cloves with a generous dash of olive oil, a pinch of salt, cayenne pepper and a splash of red wine vinegar until you have a smooth soup. Chill in the fridge.
- To poach the remaining eggs, bring a pan of water to the boil. Grease some cling film and place in a cup. Break one egg into the cup.
- Carefully lift out the cling film with the egg and tie a knot to enclose the egg. Repeat with the other 3 eggs. Place the eggs in the hot water and cook for about 3 minutes until the whites are set.
- Spoon the soup into four bowls, then unwrap the poached eggs and place one in the middle of each bowl.
- Finish with the anchovy fillets and a sprinkling of cayenne pepper to serve.

DEEP-FRIED POTATO SKINS WITH ANCHOVY DIP

SNACK/STARTER
SERVES 4

THIS is a great snack to make when you have potato skins left over from another dish. Make plenty as it is very more-ish.

4 tbsp mayonnaise
6 anchovy fillets, mashed
8 rosemary leaves, finely
*   chopped*
olive oil

4 handfuls of potato skins
sea salt and freshly ground
*   white pepper*
a sprig of rosemary, to garnish

- Mix the mayonnaise with the anchovies and rosemary, then season with a little white pepper.
- Heat about 5cm/2in olive oil in a heavy-based pan to 170°C/325°F.
- Fry the potato skins until crisp and golden brown.
- Remove the skins from the oil and drain on kitchen paper.
- Season the skins with sea salt and serve with the dip.

ANCHOVIES WITH GNOCCHI AND SAGE

MAIN COURSE
SERVES 4

1 tin of anchovy fillets in olive oil (50g/1¾oz), drained
milk (to desalt the anchovy)
250g/9oz butter

1 bunch of sage, leaves separated
500g/1lb 2oz gnocchi
1 tbsp chopped flat-leaf parsley
freshly ground white pepper

- Soak the anchovy fillets for a few minutes in lukewarm water or milk. Drain and pat dry.
- To clarify the butter, put the butter in a saucepan over a medium heat and leave to melt completely, without allowing it to brown.
- Remove the pan from the heat. With a spoon, remove the milk solids from the butter.
- Place the pan back over a medium heat and fry the sage leaves in the butter until crispy.
- Remove the pan from the heat, take out the leaves and leave to drain on kitchen paper.
- Cook the gnocchi in boiling water according to the package instructions.
- Portion the gnocchi out onto four plates. Pour over the sage butter and sprinkle with parsley and pepper.
- Add the crispy sage leaves and anchovy to the gnocchi and serve immediately.

BEEF TENDERLOIN WITH CHIMICHURRI

MAIN COURSE
SERVES 4

CHIMICHURRI is a spicy Argentinean sauce served with red meat. In this version, the anchovy and tomato paste add depth of flavour.

600g/1lb 5oz beef tenderloin, cut into large pieces
2 red chillies, cut lengthways and deseeded
olive oil
2 tbsp tomato purée
1 tsp coarse sea salt
2 tsp black pepper (preferably first dry-roasted in a frying pan)

8 garlic cloves, peeled and crushed
2 tsp chopped oregano
2 sprigs of flat-leaf parsley
6 anchovy fillets
2 tsp red wine vinegar
skewers

- Take the meat out of the fridge half an hour before cooking. If you are using wooden or bamboo skewers, put them in cold water to soak.
- In a frying pan, bring about 5mm/¼in of water to the boil. Turn down the heat once it starts boiling, add the red chillies and boil for 5 minutes.
- Remove the chillies from the water and pat dry. Cut the flesh from the skin.
- Heat a splash of olive oil in a frying pan. Turn down the heat and fry off the tomato purée for 1 minute, stirring continuously.
- Put the salt, black pepper and garlic cloves in a mortar. Bash until you have a thick paste. Add the red chilli, the herbs and the anchovies and work into the paste. Add the tomato purée and the red wine vinegar.
- Thread the meat onto skewers and season with salt.
- Cook the meat on a hot grill for about 3 minutes in total, turning frequently, or until cooked to your liking.
- Serve the meat with the chimichurri sauce.

ANCHOVY AND OLIVE TART (PISSALADIÈRE)

MAIN COURSE
SERVES 4

1 tin of anchovy fillets in olive
  oil (50g/1¾oz), drained
olive oil
2 brown onions, chopped
1 tsp sugar
1 roll ready-made puff pastry
100g/3½oz black olives, pitted
  and halved

100g/3½oz Gruyère cheese,
  grated
1 egg yolk, lightly beaten
salt and freshly ground black
  pepper

- Preheat the oven to 180°C/350°F/gas 4.
- Soak the anchovies in cold water for a few minutes to remove excess salt. Drain and lightly pat dry.
- Heat a splash of olive oil in a frying pan. Add the onions and sugar and fry over a medium heat until lightly browned.
- Remove the onions from the heat and season with salt and pepper.
- Take the puff pastry and cut out a rectangle of 25cm/10in wide (or the width of the roll) by 40cm/16in long. Fold 1cm/½in of the edge over twice to make a case.
- Spread the onions in the pastry case. Place the anchovies diagonally across the top. Sprinkle the olives and cheese over the top. Brush the pastry edges with the beaten egg yolk.
- Bake the anchovy tart in the oven for 15–20 minutes until crisp and golden brown. Serve hot or warm.

SPECIES	Mussels
BINOMIAL NAME	*Mytilus edulis*
FISHING METHODS	Small-scale dredging
MSC CERTIFIED	Among others, Scottish Mussels, Limfjord (Denmark), Oosterschelde (The Netherlands), Northern Ireland (for more information on the MSC see page 152)
TINNED OPTIONS	Mussels in water, mussels in mustard-dill, mussels in chilli-mango, smoked mussels

TO RETAIN FLAVOUR, ONLY ADD MUSSELS TO A DISH AT THE LAST MINUTE.

MUSSELS

WHEREVER there are mussels, there will be plenty of mussel farmers. They gather the mussel seed from the mussel beds and transfer them to their own plots where they are cultivated to the desired size. Sustainable mussel-seed fishermen can be found in Zeeland in The Netherlands, the South-West of England and the Limfjord in Denmark. Their sustainable method is necessary, as mussel seed is becoming scarcer in many territories, like the Dutch Wadden Sea. The still-prevalent dredging method – in which heavy chain nets scrape the sea bed – damages the natural habitats of other sea creatures. Alternative methods like the Zeeland fishermen's mussel seed-gathering systems are not just incredibly resourceful, their payoff is also very promising. The mussel seed is caught using net and rope structures and transported to the mussel plots at the bottom of the Eastern Scheldt in Zeeland, where over a few years they mature into delicious morsels.

THIS mussel seed gathering technique is similar to that of the Spanish mussel fishers. Off the Galician coast, the fishermen build wooden structures with ropes. The mussel seed attaches itself to the ropes and is harvested when the mussels have grown large enough. It is also worth mentioning the pilings method, or bouchot technique, that is used off the coasts of Normandy and Brittany in France. There, during low tide, the mussel farmers attach cylindrical nets filled with mussel seed to poles on sandbanks out on the coast. Once the mussel seed has fully grown, the mussels are then harvested and presented to the consumer as *moules de bouchots*.

THE larger-sized mussels will find their way to the consumer fresh in the shell but a large part of the harvest will be preserved in tins and jars. Tinned mussels can come from anywhere and they will generally hold the smaller mussels. Producers who add the MSC-certification to their tins often include the fishing method and location on the packaging. Most other suppliers only include the prescribed number code, which at least ensures traceability.

MUSSELS in sauce are ready to eat as they are, savoured with a simple chunk of bread. To retain the flavour when cooking mussels, only add them to a dish at the last minute.

MODERN TRADITIONAL FISHING TECHNIQUES DO THE JOB

MANY Danish fishermen sail from Nybøking harbour to the Limfjord in their colourful boats. They mostly sail alone, so the catch will be worth it financially. Poul Kaergaard takes a different approach; his two boats are manned by Erik and Mogens. They usually set out at 2 a.m. and come back around 4 p.m. the same day. They follow strict, self-imposed rules and only fish in areas of the fjord where the mussel population is strong, and they often collaborate with biologists doing research in the area. This method works: after generations of mussel fishing, the mussel beds are still in a healthy condition and their sustainable approach was awarded the MSC-certified label. To receive the MSC certification, the fishermen didn't need to change their way of fishing as their traditional fishing techniques already met the requirements perfectly.

SPANISH TOMATO RICE WITH MUSSELS

MAIN COURSE
SERVES 4

olive oil
2 peppers, deseeded and cut into
    strips
150g/5½oz soft chorizo, sliced
2 large onions, cut in pieces
1 tbsp tomato purée
300g/10½oz/heaped 1½ cups
    Spanish paella rice
1 glass of dry white wine
8 garlic cloves, peeled and cut
    into large chunks

4 ripe vine tomatoes, skinned,
    deseeded and cut into
    pieces
1.5l/52fl oz/6½ cups chicken
    stock
1 tin of mussels in a spicy
    tomato sauce (120g/4¼oz)
freshly ground black pepper
juice of 1 lemon
1 bunch of coriander, chopped

- Heat the olive oil in a frying pan and fry the peppers over a high heat for about 1 minute, stirring all the time. Remove from the pan and set aside.
- Reheat the pan and fry the chorizo over a medium heat for a few minutes on each side. Remove from the pan and set aside.
- Pour the released oils out of the pan, but don't clean the pan.
- Gently fry the onions in the remaining chorizo oil.
- Add the tomato purée to the onion and cook for 1 minute.
- Add the rice and fry for 1 minute, stirring occasionally.
- Pour the wine into the pan and bring to the boil, stirring for 1 minute.
- Add the garlic, tomatoes and reserved peppers with enough of the chicken stock to just cover the rice. Bring to a simmer and simmer gently over a low heat, stirring, until the stock has been absorbed.
- Add the remaining stock a little at a time, stirring, until the rice is just tender and the stock has been absorbed. The cooking time should be about 18 minutes (also see the packet instructions on the rice).
- When the rice is almost cooked, stir in the reserved chorizo and warm through, then add the mussels, black pepper and lemon juice to taste.
- Serve on four deep plates, garnished with the coriander.

MUSSEL ESCABÈCHE WITH ROASTED PEPPERS

STARTER
SERVES 4

THIS is probably the simplest, cheapest and tastiest recipe in this book. When you're in a Spanish food shop or a good fishmonger, do stock up on a couple of tins of *mejillones en escabeche*. They keep for years, so if you like the dish it's worth buying a few. Escabèche is a spicy Spanish marinade made with paprika, pepper and vinegar or lemon. The sour taste goes well with the sweet mussels.

4 red peppers
3 tins of mussels in escabèche
     sauce (120g/4¼oz per tin)
2 tbsp mayonnaise

1 garlic clove, peeled and
     crushed
4 slices of white bread, toasted

- Preheat the grill.
- Cut the peppers in half lengthways. Place them cut-side down on greaseproof paper on the grill rack so that any excess liquid can flow freely. Put under the grill and cook, turning once, until both sides are blistered and blackened but the flesh is still soft and juicy.
- Remove from the grill and put in a sealed plastic bag to cool. When cool, remove the skin and seeds.
- Using a fork, mash the pepper flesh with the oil from one tin of mussels, the mayonnaise and the garlic.
- Stir in the mussels.
- Serve spread on the toast.

SPECIES	Chum salmon, pink salmon and sockeye salmon
BINOMIAL NAME	*Oncorhynchus keta, Oncorhynchus gorbuscha* and *Oncorhynchus nerka*
FISHING METHODS	Drift nets and purse seine
MSC CERTIFIED	All salmon fisheries in Alaska (US) and Canada, various in Russia (for more information on the MSC see page 152)
TINNED OPTIONS	Salmon in water, skinless and boneless salmon in water

ALASKAN FISHERIES HAVE BEEN WORKING UNDER STRICT CATCH REGULATIONS SINCE 1959.

SALMON

WHEN it comes to tinned salmon, more and more varieties are becoming available: wild pink salmon, wild red salmon and farmed salmon, for example. The producer can also include the species on the label, which can be useful if you prefer the flavour of one to another. It's also good to know whether or not the salmon has been preserved with the bones. Heat softens the nutritious bones and makes them digestible. The skin is often also preserved in the tin with the salmon.

WILD salmon have to swim a lot during their lifetime and that shows through in the flesh, as the fat is more evenly distributed compared to farmed salmon. The wild salmon's firm flesh also generally has a stronger flavour. Farmed salmon can be found all over the world and European farming pools hold Atlantic salmon (*Salmo salar*) but it is highly unlikely you'll find Atlantic salmon in your tin as most tinned salmon is wild salmon from the coastal waters and rivers of Alaska. These seas and rivers are some of the cleanest in the world, which is important as the salmon's fat easily retains impurities.

BECAUSE the fisheries have been working under strict catch regulations since 1959, the existence of the Alaskan salmon is not threatened. For years, scientists and fishermen – often Inuit – have been keeping track of how many salmon swim to the spawning grounds each year. Based on these numbers, they determine the catch. This approach has earned them the coveted MSC certification.

FIVE types of salmon that are known by the general public under their native name are caught during the season: the light pink chum or keta salmon (*Oncorhynchus keta*) is generally the cheapest. The humpback salmon (*Oncorhynchus gorbuscha*) is sold as pink salmon. The coho or silver salmon (*Oncorhynchus kisutch*) is important to fishermen because of the high price they fetch. The best salmon swim up river in the spring. The fatty sockeye (*Oncorhynchus nerka*) or red salmon is available freshly smoked as well as tinned. The chinook or king salmon (*Oncorhynchus tshawytscha*) is the largest of the salmon family and those caught are mainly destined for the smokehouses.

CHUM FROM THE YUKON AND PINK FROM THE POLAR STAR

IN Alaska, both the indigenous people and other Americans fish for salmon with an MSC certification and are bound by strict catch regulations. In summer, Yup'ik Eskimo Maxine casts her nets from her small boat into the fast-flowing Yukon, in the hope of catching lots of chum salmon which, according to Maxine, is the best salmon available.

ONE of the 6,200 inhabitants of Kodiak Island, Pat Pikus takes a different approach to salmon fishing: he sails out to open sea and uses ring nets. Fellow fishermen see Pat as one of the best salmon fishermen in Alaska. He catches pink salmon, sailing his family's boat the Polar Star. The fishermen name the pink salmon after a village at the foot of the narrow Aleutian mountain range, an isthmus reaching a different time zone in the Pacific Ocean. Fishermen like Pat, who use ring nets in this part of Alaska, strictly adhere to the catch restrictions. A portion of his catch is destined for the Ocean Beauty cannery in Seattle, the same cannery where the Fish Tales tins are manufactured. Salmon fishing on the open sea in these tempestuous parts of the Pacific is not without its dangers. Pat and his men regularly save people from drowning in the freezing cold water.

SALMON TARTARE WITH SOFT-BOILED EGGS AND SPRING ONIONS

Starter
serves 4

2 tins of pink or red salmon,
   boneless and skinless
   (170g/6oz drained weight
   per tin), drained
5 tbsp mayonnaise
2 eggs, soft-boiled

3 spring onions, roughly
   chopped
freshly ground black pepper
4 slices of sourdough bread,
   toasted

- Mash the salmon with the mayonnaise to make a creamy tartare, then spoon onto a plate.
- Arrange the eggs on the tartare and sprinkle with the spring onions. Season with black pepper.
- Serve with toasted sourdough bread.

SALMON, LEEK AND CREAM CHEESE QUICHE

STARTER/MAIN COURSE
SERVES 4

2 leeks, white parts only, cut in half
    lengthways and finely sliced.
1 tbsp olive oil
a dash of white wine
3 eggs, beaten
250ml/9fl oz/generous 1 cup
    whipping cream

2 tins of red or pink salmon
    (215g/7½oz per tin), drained
30g/1oz butter, melted
8 sheets of ready-rolled puff pastry
150g/5½oz cream cheese
100g/3½oz bag of mixed salad
salt and freshly ground black pepper

- Preheat the oven to 180°C/350°F/gas 4 and grease a 25cm/10in cake tin.
- Fry the leeks in the oil over a low heat until soft but not browned.
- Add the wine and bring to the boil, stirring to mix in the juices.
- Mix the eggs, cream, salmon and seasoning, then stir in the leeks.
- Line the tin with the puff pastry, prick the base with a fork and bake for 8 minutes. Remove from the oven and press to flatten the base.
- Pour the egg-cream mixture into the base and dot with the cream cheese.
- Bake for 30 minutes until set and golden brown. Serve with the salad.

POTATO AND LEEK SOUP WITH RED SALMON

Starter
serves 4

5 leeks, white parts only
50g/1¾oz butter
3 floury potatoes, such as Maris
    Piper, peeled and cut into
    chunks
400ml/14floz/1⅔ cups chicken
    stock
ice cubes
1 tin of pink or red salmon,
    boneless and skinless
    (170g/6oz drained
    weight), drained and cut
    into chunks

1 red pepper, deseeded and
    thinly sliced
1 handful of chives, finely
    chopped
salt and freshly ground white
    pepper

- Chop 4 of the leeks. The remaining leek will serve as a garnish.
- Heat the butter in a deep, heavy-based pan, add the leeks and braise until soft, without allowing them to brown.
- Add the potatoes and chicken stock to the pan, bring to a simmer and leave to cook on a low heat until the potatoes are tender.
- Meanwhile, bring a pan of water to the boil while you cut the remaining leek into thin rings. Parboil the leek in the boiling water for 1 minute, then drain and put into a bowl of iced water.
- Season the soup with salt and pepper. Heat the soup thoroughly and froth up with a stick blender.
- Spoon the soup into bowls and add the salmon, then garnish with the sliced pepper, leek rings and chives.

SALMON SPREAD WITH SOURDOUGH BREAD

STARTER/MAIN COURSE
SERVES 2–4

2 tins of pink or red salmon,
    boneless and skinless
    (170g/6oz drained weight
    per tin), drained and cut
    into chunks
3 tbsp mayonnaise
2 tbsp whipping cream, beaten
    to soft peaks

1 tsp cayenne pepper
1 tsp finely grated lemon zest
1 spring onion, thinly sliced
1 tbsp lemon juice
salt and freshly ground black
    pepper
4 slices of sourdough bread,
    toasted if you like

- Mash the salmon in a bowl. Add the mayonnaise, whipped cream and cayenne pepper and mix to a fairly smooth consistency.
- Now add the lemon zest and the spring onion. Season with lemon juice, salt and pepper.
- Spread on the sourdough slices and serve.

SPECIES	Mackerel
BINOMIAL NAME	*Scomber scombrus*
FISHING METHODS	Drift nets and purse seine
MSC CERTIFIED	The certification has been temporarily suspended, because the countries involved could not reach an agreement on quota. The stocks are healthy. More talks were held in 2014, but there is currently no clarity on whether the MSC suspension will be lifted in the near future (for more information on the MSC see page 152)
TINNED OPTIONS	Steamed mackerel in water, mackerel in oil, smoked mackerel in oil, mackerel in sauce

IN SALADS, MACKEREL IS A GOOD SUBSTITUTE FOR THE OFTEN-USED TUNA AND SALMON.

MACKEREL

In the supermarket aisles, you'll find many varieties of tinned mackerel: steamed mackerel in water, mackerel in oil, smoked mackerel in oil, mackerel in sauce, mackerel with black pepper; the fish is apparently popular. And rightly so, because the delicious, oily mackerel is a source of healthy omega-3 fatty acids and other nutrients. It is also a very versatile fish in both its natural and smoked forms and goes well with many flavours. For example, in salads mackerel is a good substitute for the often-used tuna and salmon.

Neutral flavoured pieces of mackerel fillet are initially briefly sterilised with a small amount of salt. To make mackerel in sauce, the fish processors first place the mackerel in a brine and then steam the fish in a tin without a lid. It is then drained of excess water, the tin is filled with a sauce and covered with a lid. The tins are then sterilised. Even smoked mackerel is first brined before being smoked in a smoking chamber, after which the oil is added. The tin is then covered and ready for sterilisation.

JAPAN produces extraordinary mackerel, prepared with ginger and typically Japanese ingredients like miso. Connoisseurs believe this mackerel is best served on its own rather than mixed with other flavours. This book doesn't feature any recipes with Japanese mackerel, although if you want to try it, it is available on the internet.

THE fat content of the mackerel depends on the fishing season, which itself varies depending on the latitude and the type of mackerel. The fish processor will take this into account because you get better

results if you smoke a fatty mackerel rather than a lean one. Mackerel from the northern hemisphere is lean around May, when the fish have just spawned. In summer and early autumn the mackerel fill themselves up with food, so from October onwards the fishermen can start to haul in these big boys.

More and more fisheries are turning to stock-saving techniques and show a willingness to return unwanted bycatch to the sea. North Atlantic mackerel fishing had been MSC-certified for years, but since 2013 the certificate has been temporarily suspended and mackerel fishermen have no longer been allowed to carry the certification label. The reason for this is that countries with uncertified fisheries, like Iceland, were also fishing the same areas, which meant that more mackerel was being caught than had been agreed in the quotas. Negotiations are necessary to ensure that fisheries will all adhere to the requirements. Having said that, the mackerel populations in these areas is nonetheless healthy.

MACKEREL WITH STIR-FRIED VEGETABLES AND CHILLI SAUCE

MAIN COURSE
SERVES 4

*200g/7oz sugar snap peas or
  mangetout*
*200g/7oz broccolini, cut
  lengthways*
about 2 tbsp sesame oil
2 onions, chopped
1 tsp soy sauce

*2 tins of mackerel fillet in olive
  oil (125g/4½oz drained
  weight per tin), drained*
50g/1¾oz leek sprouts
chilli sauce
freshly ground black pepper

- Bring a pan of lightly salted water to the boil, add the sugar snap peas and boil for a few minutes until just tender, then drain, reserving the water.
- Return it to the boil and blanch the broccolini in the same way. Drain and pat dry.
- Put a wok over a high heat, add a dash of sesame oil and fry the onions until golden brown. Remove them from the wok.
- Add a little more sesame oil to the pan and fry the sugar snaps and broccolini on a high heat until hot and coated in oil.
- Add the fried onions and stir, then add the soy sauce and stir everything together until hot.
- Remove the wok from the heat and season the vegetables with black pepper.
- Divide the vegetables among four plates and place the mackerel on top of the vegetables.
- Add the leek sprouts and serve with chilli sauce.

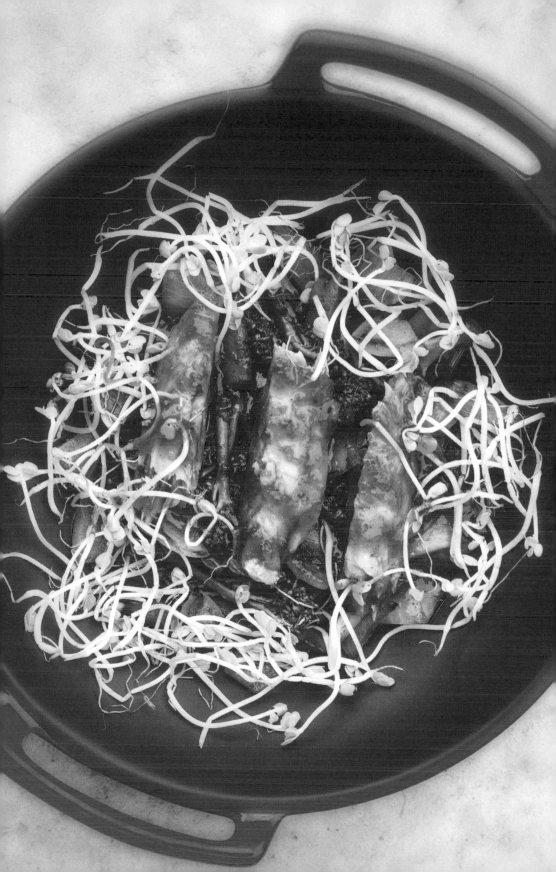

PEKING MACKEREL

Snack/starter
Serves 4

2 little gem lettuces
1 jar of hoisin sauce (210g/7oz)
1 ripe mango, in small slices
1 cucumber, peeled, deseeded
    and cut into thin strips
1 bunch of spring onions, white
    parts only, cut into thin
    strips

1 tin of smoked mackerel fillet,
    (125g/4½oz drained weight
    per can), drained and
    flaked
1 small piece of fresh root ginger,
    peeled and grated

- Remove the outer leaves of the little gems, then remove the hearts, to create little cups.
- In each lettuce cup, spoon 1 teaspoon of hoisin sauce.
- Place a slice of mango in each cup. Add the strips of cucumber and spring onion.
- Add the pieces of mackerel to the cups.
- To finish, sprinkle a little of the grated ginger on top of the mackerel.

SMOKED MACKEREL, MASH AND PICCALILLI

STARTER
SERVES 4

400g/14oz potatoes
100g/3½oz cold butter, cut into
    cubes
100ml/3½fl oz/scant ½ cup hot
    milk
sea salt

a pinch of freshly grated nutmeg
1 tin of smoked mackerel fillet
    (125g/4½oz drained
    weight), drained
1 jar of piccalilli

- Bring a large pan of water to the boil and boil the potatoes in their skins until just tender.
- Drain, leave until cool enough to handle, then peel the potatoes, reserving the skins for Deep-Fried Potato Skins with Anchovy Dip on page 54.
- Mash the potato flesh with a potato ricer or masher, then beat in the cold butter with a spatula, then stir in the hot milk. Season with salt and nutmeg.
- Ladle the mash onto four plates.
- Place the pieces of mackerel on top and serve with piccalilli.

SMOKED MACKEREL WITH BRAISED LEEKS

STARTER
SERVES 4

25g/10z/scant ¼ cup pine nuts
4 medium-sized leeks, white
    base only
olive oil
100ml/3½fl oz/scant ½ cup
    chicken stock
3 tbsp white wine vinegar
3 tbsp sunflower oil

1 tbsp Dijon mustard
2 tins of smoked mackerel fillets
    (125g/4½oz per tin)
a few sprigs of tarragon
salt and freshly ground black
    pepper

- Heat a frying pan and dry roast the pine nuts for a few minutes until lightly browned. Set aside.
- Remove the outer leaves of the leeks. Rinse and remove any sand. Cut the leeks in half and then cut in half lengthways.
- Heat a generous splash of olive oil in a frying pan. Turn the heat down to low and place the leeks cut-side down in the oil.
- Add a splash of chicken stock and leave the leeks to cook gently for about 15 minutes until they are tender when pierced with a sharp knife, turning once during cooking.
- Put the vinegar, sunflower oil, mustard, salt and pepper in a bowl and beat with a fork or whisk into a vinaigrette.
- Divide the leeks among four plates. Place the mackerel on top of the leeks and spoon the vinaigrette over the dish.
- Garnish with pine nuts and tarragon leaves.

MACKEREL WITH WATERCRESS AND LEEKS

MAIN COURSE
SERVES 4

200g/7oz waxy potatoes
olive oil
2 tbsp white wine vinegar
1 tbsp Dijon mustard
100g/3½oz bag of watercress
2 tins of mackerel fillets in olive
    oil (125g/4½oz per tin),
    drained

50g/1¾oz leek sprouts
sea salt and freshly ground
    white pepper

- Bring a large pan of water to the boil and boil the potatoes in their skins until just tender.
- Drain, then roughly crush the potatoes with a drizzle of olive oil and season with salt and pepper.
- Put the vinegar, a splash of olive oil, the mustard and a pinch of salt in a bowl and whisk into a vinaigrette.
- Toss the watercress with the vinaigrette and place on four plates. Add the crushed potatoes, then the mackerel and garnish with the leek sprouts.

MACKEREL, BEETROOT, APPLE AND PICKLE REMOULADE

2 tbsp Dijon mustard
1 tbsp red wine vinegar, plus
    extra for seasoning
a dash of Worcestershire sauce
4 tbsp olive oil
1 shallot, finely chopped
2 cooked beetroots
1 crisp green eating apple, such
    as a Granny Smith

2 pickled gherkins
250ml/9fl oz/generous 1 cup
    soured cream
2 tbsp finely chopped chives
2 tins of smoked mackerel
    fillet (125g/4½oz per tin),
    drained and flaked
salt and freshly ground black
    pepper

- Use a fork to beat the mustard, vinegar, Worcestershire sauce, olive oil and shallot into a vinaigrette, seasoning with salt and pepper.
- Cut the beetroot, apple and pickle into 5mm/¼in cubes.
- Add the vinaigrette to the cubes and season with salt and pepper, if necessary.
- Mix the soured cream with some salt, pepper, a few drops of red wine vinegar and the chives. Stir in the smoked mackerel.
- Put equal amounts of the smoked mackerel and beetroot on four plates and serve.

SPECIES	Sardine
BINOMIAL NAME	*Sardina pilchardus*
FISHING METHODS	Purse seine
MSC CERTIFIED	South-Brittany (France) and Cornwall (UK) (for more information on the MSC see page 152). Portugese sardine fishery temporarily suspended while stocks recover..
TINNED OPTIONS	Sardines in water, sardines in olive oil, sardines in tomato sauce, sardine fillets in olive oil

THE PORTUGUESE CONSIDER THEIR TINNED SARDINES TO BE THE ABSOLUTE FINEST.

SARDINES

SARDINES come in all sizes. On land they are arranged in size in factories by skilful hands or machines so that similarly sized sardines are tinned together. The larger sardines that don't fit in the small tins after decapitation will be cut into pieces and processed as fillets. The really tiny ones are used in spreads or as fish feed.

FANS of these little squirts won't be forgotten. Some producers offer them as *sardinella*, a delicious tapas dish. In a bar somewhere in Spain, after a glass of white wine, you can get into a heated discussion about sardines. Is the *sardinella* actually a sardine? The barman will set you straight: of course it's a real sardine. After all it's a member of the same family – the mouth of the sardine doesn't extend as far as its cousin's, the anchovy. He'll be able to tell you about *sardinops* (South American pilchards) and that the English regard the pilchard as the true sardine. And sardines are also related to herring, he'll add. You could find yourself entering a seemingly endless discussion, so it's probably advisable to leave scientific classification as a topic and steer the conversation into a culinary direction – which is hard enough, because how should you serve sardines as a tapas dish? One person swears by lemon, the other prefers the fish with the finest olive oil. And why not add a *salsa picante*?

SARDINES have been tinned for nearly 200 years. In the nineteenth century the tinned fish was regarded as a delicacy by the upper classes. Because the soft fish disintegrated almost immediately when picked out of the tin with a fork, a cutlery manufacturer developed the sardine fork with blunt prongs, and collectors will readily pay high prices for antique examples. A well-conserved sardine fork even got a display spot in the Central Museum of Utrecht.

A few European countries have a true tradition of tinning sardines. You should buy sardines from a reputable brand, keep in a cool place outside the fridge and turn regularly to ensure the fish doesn't dry out on one side.

ACCORDING to the French, sardines were first tinned along the south coast of Brittany, and there are still many factories along the coast making tinned sardines, often in sauce. One of the oldest recipes is *sardines au beurre*, often a *beurre de baratte*, a farmhouse butter. A typically French custom is to heat the tin in hot water, then open it and eat the sardines with more melted butter, baby potatoes and lettuce. Another French tradition is to mature the sardines in the tin, which enhances the flavour of the fish.

THE treatment of the sardines also determines the quality of the tinned product. In this respect, North-Portuguese producer A Poveira sets the standards by his good practice. The Portuguese consider their tinned sardines to be the absolute best. A Poveira only uses the freshest sardines that come in daily and are cut and tinned by hand in the workshop (also see page 18).

SARDINE levels are healthy in certain waters. To ensure the continuing safety of the stock populations, a number of fisheries – from Cornwall and South Brittany to name a few – had themselves certified by the MSC. These fisheries operate under catch restrictions and strict fishing methods.

SARDINES AND BURRATA WITH ROASTED VEGETABLES

STARTER
SERVES 4

USE the best-quality burrata, if you can, made with buffalo mozzarella and cream. If you can't get burrata, use buffalo mozzarella or ordinary mozzarella.

1 courgette, sliced
1 red pepper, deseeded and sliced
1 yellow pepper, deseeded and
    sliced
1 aubergine, sliced
2 red onions, quartered
olive oil
1 soft chorizo (or a 10cm/4in
    piece of hard chorizo), cut
    into chunks

250g/9oz cherry tomatoes
3 garlic cloves, roughly chopped
1 burrata or mozzarella, diced
    or crumbled
2 tins of sardines in water or
    olive oil (120g/4¼oz each),
    drained
coarse sea salt and freshly
    ground black pepper
1 lemon, cut into wedges

- Preheat the oven to 180°C/350°F/gas 4.
- Drizzle all the vegetables with olive oil and roast for 20 minutes.
- Meanwhile, heat a splash of olive oil in a frying pan and fry the chorizo for a moment. Remove from the pan and drain half of the released oils. Set the chorizo aside.
- Fry the tomatoes and chopped garlic in the fatty juices over a medium heat until just softened.
- Remove the tomatoes from the heat and return the chorizo to the pan.
- Place the vegetables, tomatoes and chorizo on a large plate.
- Place the burrata or mozzarella on the vegetables.
- Season with sea salt and black pepper.
- Serve with the sardines and lemon wedges.

SARDINE AND TWO-CHEESE CROSTINI

SNACK/STARTER
SERVES 4

1 tin of sardines in water or olive
    oil (120g/4¼oz), drained
200g/7oz cherry tomatoes
olive oil
1 tsp tomato purée
1 onion, chopped
1 tsp balsamic vinegar
a couple of cabbage leaves
100g/3½oz wild spinach, rinsed
    and dried

grilled or toasted baguette slices
100g/3½oz Parmesan cheese,
    shaved
100g/3½oz tangy soft goat's
    cheese, crumbled
salt and freshly ground black
    pepper
a few chives, finely chopped

- Mash the sardines with a fork, then cover and set aside in the fridge.
- Cut the cherry tomatoes in half and remove the seeds.
- Heat a splash of olive oil in a frying pan and stir in the tomato purée.
- Place the tomatoes, cut-side down, in the oil. Add the onion and balsamic vinegar. Turn down the heat and leave the tomatoes until the skins are shrivelled and the cut side has coloured slightly. Remove the pan from the heat and leave the tomatoes to cool.
- Gently remove the skins from the tomatoes.
- Roughly crush the tomatoes with the onion and oil. Season with salt and pepper.
- Cut and remove the centre vein of the cabbage leaves and cut the leaves into strips. Heat a splash of olive oil in a large frying pan and quickly cook the cabbage on a high heat until just wilted.
- Heat a splash of olive oil in a second large frying pan and quickly cook the spinach on a high heat. Drain off any excess liquid, if necessary.
- Place the tomato salsa on some of the crostini. Lay the sardines and cabbage leaf on the tomatoes and sprinkle with Parmesan cheese.
- Place the remaining sardines on the other crostini, add some spinach and goat's cheese and garnish with chives.

TARTARE OF SARDINE WITH TOMATO CARPACCIO

STARTER
SERVES 4

2 tins of sardines in olive oil
    (120g/4¼oz each), drained
2 tbsp capers, rinsed and finely
    chopped
3 tbsp sundried tomatoes, finely
    chopped
3 tbsp pitted black olives, finely
    chopped
1 bunch of basil leaves, torn

2 red vine tomatoes, sliced
2 orange tomatoes, sliced
2 yellow tomatoes, sliced
2 green tomatoes, sliced
50g/1¾oz soft goat's cheese
good-quality olive oil
sea salt and freshly ground
    white pepper

- Using a fork, mash the sardines, then mix with the capers, sundried tomatoes, olives and some finely chopped basil leaves to create the tartare.
- Place the tartare in the middle of a large plate.
- Arrange the tomato slices around the tartare.
- Crumble the goat's cheese over the tomatoes and sprinkle with some basil.
- Drizzle some olive oil over the tomatoes.
- Season with sea salt and white pepper to finish.

SARDINES WITH CONFIT THYME TOMATOES

MOST dried garlic has a sulphuric smell, which is not good for this dish. Fresh garlic, also known as wet garlic, is available from July onwards. This garlic is milder in smell and taste compared to dried garlic and will not easily overpower a dish. The wet garlic is available until mid-December, due to a preserving method in oxygen-depleted cooling cells.

200g/7oz cherry tomatoes
olive oil
8 garlic cloves, peeled and
*   roughly chopped*
a few sprigs of thyme, finely
*   chopped*

½ tsp balsamic vinegar
2 tins of sardines or sardinella
*   in olive oil (120g/4¼oz*
*   each), drained*
sea salt and freshly ground
*   black pepper*

- Cut the cherry tomatoes in half and remove the seeds.
- Heat the olive oil in a large frying pan and place the tomatoes, cut-side down, into the pan. Add the garlic and a little thyme. Turn down the heat and leave the tomatoes to slowly absorb the flavours.
- Once the skins are shrivelled and the cut side has coloured slightly, remove the pan from the heat and leave the tomatoes to cool.
- Gently remove the skins from the tomatoes. This should be easy if the tomatoes are completely cooked.
- Crush the tomatoes with the garlic and olive oil. Season with the vinegar, salt and pepper.
- Spoon the tomatoes on to plates, top with sardines or *sardinella* and sprinkle with a little more thyme, if you like.

SARDINES WITH PAPAS AND MOJO

STARTER
SERVES 4

2 sweet pointed peppers
3 red chillies
2 tsp cumin seeds
1 tsp coriander seeds
8 garlic cloves, peeled and
    chopped
olive oil
2 tbsp red wine vinegar
1 tsp paprika powder

100g/3½oz sea salt, plus extra
    for seasoning
100ml/3½fl oz/scant ½ cup
    water
250g/9oz baby potatoes in their
    skins
2 tins of sardines in olive oil
    (120g/4¼oz each), drained

- Preheat the grill.
- Cut the sweet pointed peppers in half and remove the seeds, place them on a rack with the skin-side up and grill until the skin has blistered and blackened and the flesh is soft. Cover and leave to cool.
- Remove the skin and cut the flesh into thin strips. Set aside.
- Fill a small frying pan with water and bring to the boil. Remove the green stalks from the red chillies. Cut them lengthways and remove the seeds. Place the chillies in the water and cook for a few minutes until soft.
- Remove the chillies from the water and pat dry. Scrape the flesh from the skin with a knife.
- Heat a frying pan and dry roast the cumin and coriander seeds for a minute or so.
- Using a pestle and mortar, grind the cumin and coriander seeds, then mix them with the peppers, chillies, garlic cloves and a generous dash of olive oil. Season with the vinegar, some more olive oil, paprika powder and a pinch of salt. Set the mojo aside.
- Add the salt to a pan of boiling water and cook the baby potatoes until tender. Remove the potatoes from the water using a slotted spoon and leave to cool. They're ready to eat when a coated with a white salt residue.
- Serve the potatoes with the mojo and the sardines.

SARDINE AND GARLIC MASH

SNACK/STARTER
SERVES 4

1 garlic bulb
4 tbsp olive oil, plus extra for
    drizzling
150g/5oz potatoes, peeled
4 eggs
2 tins of sardines in water or
    olive oil (120g/4¼oz each),
    drained

1 tbsp chopped flat-leaf parsley
1 tbsp lemon juice
sea salt and freshly ground black
    pepper
crusty bread

- Preheat the oven to 180°C/350°F/gas 4.
- Wrap the bulb of garlic with a couple of drops of olive oil in kitchen foil. Roast the garlic for 30–40 minutes until soft. Gently squeeze the cloves out of the papery skin. Use four or however many you like. Keep the rest to use in other dishes.
- Boil the potatoes in salted water until tender, then drain.
- Meanwhile, boil the eggs for 8 minutes, then drain, rinse in cold water and leave to cool.
- Roughly crush the potatoes with a fork.
- Peel the eggs and mash with a fork.
- Mash the sardines with a fork.
- Combine the potatoes, eggs and sardines with the olive oil and most of the parsley. Season with lemon juice, salt and pepper.
- Garnish with garlic cloves, sprinkle with the remaining parsley and serve with crusty bread.

SARDINE BITES WITH WHITE BEAN PURÉE AND BASIL OIL

SNACK/STARTER
SERVES 4

10 fresh basil leaves
3 tbsp olive oil
sea salt
a splash of lime juice
250g/9oz tinned butter beans,
    drained
1 tbsp mayonnaise
3 tbsp olive oil
10 sundried tomatoes, finely
    chopped

2 tins of sardines in water or
    olive oil (120g/4¼oz each),
    drained
thin crispbreads
sea salt and freshly ground
    black pepper
a few basil leaves, to garnish

- First make the basil oil. Using a food processor or stick blender, mix the basil leaves and oil. (If you use a pestle and mortar to combine the basil with some salt, pepper and oil, it will result in a creamier texture and flavour.)
- Season further with some lime juice.
- Put the beans in a colander and rinse. Leave to drain. Purée the beans with the mayonnaise and olive oil.
- Stir in the sundried tomatoes. Season with salt and pepper.
- Place the sardines on the crispbreads.
- Top with the white bean purée, drizzle some basil oil over the top and sprinkle with sea salt. Garnish with some torn basil leaves.

SARDINE BITES WITH CHICKPEA PURÉE AND ROASTED GARLIC

SNACK/STARTER
SERVES 4

25 garlic cloves, peeled
olive oil
1 red onion, chopped
250g/9oz cooked chickpeas,
    rinsed and drained
sesame oil
grated zest and juice of 1 lime

2 tins of sardines in water or
    olive oil (120g/4¼oz),
    drained
sea salt and freshly ground
    black pepper
thin crispbreads
cayenne pepper

- Preheat the oven to 180°C/350°F/gas 4.
- Put the garlic cloves in a piece of kitchen foil, drizzle with some olive oil and season with salt and pepper. Fold over the top and roast for 20 minutes until completely soft. Squeeze one of the cloves to check that they are done. Remove the parcel from the oven.
- Heat a splash of olive oil in a frying pan and fry the onion over a medium heat until just coloured. Remove from the pan and set aside.
- Put the chickpeas in a bowl and add 5 roasted garlic cloves. Mix into a loose purée with a dash of sesame oil, some lime juice, and salt and pepper to taste.
- Roughly mash the sardines with a dash of olive oil.
- Place the onions on the crispbreads and top with the sardines.
- Spoon some chickpea purée onto the sardines and press the roasted garlic cloves into the purée.
- To finish, garnish the crispbreads with some sea salt, cayenne pepper and lime zest.

SPECIES	Snow crab and red king crab
BINOMIAL NAME	*Pralithodes camtschatius* and *Chionoecetes opilio*
FISHING METHODS	Traps and pots
MSC CERTIFIED	Nova Scotia, Gulf of St Lawrence and Newfoundland & Labrador (Canada) (for more information on the MSC see page 152)
TINNED OPTIONS	Crabmeat in water

CRABMEAT FROM THE CLAWS IS FLAVOURSOME AND WELL SUITED TO SOUPS AND SAUCES.

CRAB

THE red king crab is the only crab whose name is proudly used on the labels of tins. This has to do with the limited supply available of this crab. The crab – with its claws like garden shears – hails from Alaskan waters and is the star of the popular Discovery Channel programme *Deadliest Catch*. American fishermen bring in these sturdy crabs, frequently measuring more than a metre in size, from the freezing Bering Sea. The crab is very profitable, so the fishermen literally cram as many as they can into the hold.

THE red king crab finds its way to the consumer both fresh and frozen, but also in tins and jars. The Russians also catch this crab and most of their meat is destined for the Chatka cannery in Spain. Hunks of red king crabmeat will be an assault on your weekly shopping budget – tinned crab doesn't get better than this, although this level of quality comes at a price. Several producers specialising in fish are particularly known for supplying tins with crab of this quality.

OTHER countries, however, like Chile, export more competitively priced tinned red king crab. In some areas, you can also buy cheaper tinned crabmeat, commonly known as 'extra fancy' or 'special', which contains some claw meat. This crab comes from Southeast Asia. Fancy crabmeat is perfectly fine to drain and use in crab cakes, soups, salads and quesadillas.

COUNTRIES where a lot of crab is consumed offer meat of varying quality. Lump, one large piece or several slightly smaller pieces, is the highest quality, then special, which might be of lower quality but is preferable in taste and structure to surimi, imitation crabmeat made from pressed white fish meat. Producers also offer just meat from the claws, which is darker in colour and very flavoursome. This meat is well suited to soups and sauces.

CRAB is also available to the consumer in both MSC-certified and uncertified tins. Crab from certified fisheries in Canada will partly be sold with the blue MSC label.

GOOD-QUALITY snow crab is available from the fishermen of the Canadian Nova Scotia peninsula. The smaller snow crab is also quite expensive. The fishermen catch the crabs in cage traps. Part of the catch won't leave the island – tourists eat the crabs in restaurants along one the world's most beautiful coastal roads, the Cabot Trail. The tranquil Nova Scotia has so much to offer, you find yourself wondering why people go out to sea. It must be the fishermen's hunting instinct.

PLANTAIN, CRAB AND MANGO CHUTNEY

FOR a tasty alternative, use smoked mackerel, smoked mussels or kippers instead of crab.

1 tin of crabmeat (170g/6oz), drained	sunflower oil
1 tbsp mayonnaise	1 jar of mango chutney, preferably Sharwood's
1 lime	cayenne pepper
1 plantain	a few chives, finely chopped
1 tbsp plain flour, sifted	crispy fried onions, to garnish

- Mix the crab with the mayonnaise and a few drops of lime juice.
- Cut the plantain into 6mm (about $1/4$in) thick slices.
- Put the flour on a sheet of cling film. Flour both sides of the plantain slices and place them on the cling film. Place another layer of cling film on top. Use a pan to press down lightly on the plantain to make the slices a bit thinner.
- Heat a little oil in a large frying pan and fry the slices until crisp and golden brown. This should take about a minute.
- Use kitchen paper to pat dry and drain excess oil.
- Place a teaspoon of mango chutney on each slice.
- Spoon the crab on top of the mango chutney.
- Sprinkle with cayenne pepper, the chives and the crispy fried onions.

CRAB SALAD WITH ORANGE AND FENNEL

Starter
serves 4

juice of 1 orange
juice of ½ lime
4 tbsp mayonnaise
3 little gems or 1 cos lettuce
2 oranges, peeled and cut in
    segments
1 baby fennel bulb, cut into thin
    strips

2 tins of crabmeat (170g/6oz
    each), drained
1 bunch of basil or Thai basil
sea salt and freshly ground
    white pepper

- Beat the orange and lime juice, the mayonnaise, salt and pepper together to make a dressing.
- Remove and discard the outer leaves of the lettuce and detach the lettuce leaves from the heart. Arrange on a plate.
- Put the orange segments, the fennel strips and the crab on the lettuce leaves.
- Drizzle the dressing over the salad and garnish with small basil leaves.

CRAB WITH APPLE AND CURRY-GINGER SAUCE

STARTER
SERVES 4

1 celery stick
3 sharp eating apples, such as
    Granny Smith
1 tin of crabmeat (170g/6oz),
    drained

1 tbsp curry powder
4 tbsp mayonnaise
1 3cm/1¼in piece of fresh root
    ginger, peeled and grated
cayenne pepper

- With a knife, pull off the tough fibrous strings of the celery stick, then cut the celery into thin crescent shapes.
- Peel an apple and cut into cubes.
- Take the crab legs from the tin and set aside.
- Mix the remaining crabmeat with the curry powder, mayonnaise, apple cubes, grated ginger and part of the celery. Season with cayenne pepper.
- From the top and bottom of the remaining two apples, cut slices about 3mm/⅛in thick.
- Place the crab salad on the apple slices. Garnish with the crab legs, some cayenne pepper and the remaining celery.

MUSHROOMS WITH CRAB, GARLIC AND GRUYÈRE

MAIN COURSE
SERVES 4

20 large white mushrooms
juice of 1 lemon
2 tins of crabmeat (170g/6oz
    each), drained
2 tbsp olive oil
1 tbsp very finely chopped garlic,
2 tbsp finely chopped flat-leaf
    parsley

cayenne pepper
100g/3½oz Gruyère cheese,
    grated
2 tbsp finely chopped chives
sea salt

- Preheat the oven to 190°C/375°F/gas 5.
- Cut the stems off the mushroom (use them later for a soup).
- Bring a large saucepan of water to the boil with the lemon juice and a pinch of salt.
- Add the mushroom caps and boil for 2 minutes.
- Remove from the pan and leave the mushrooms to drain on a tea towel.
- Combine the crab, olive oil, garlic, parsley, a pinch of cayenne pepper and, if necessary, a little salt.
- Put the mushrooms, gill-side up, in a baking pan, fill them with the crab mixture and sprinkle the grated Gruyère on top.
- Bake the mushrooms in the oven for about 7 minutes. If necessary, place under the grill to add some colour to the cheese.
- Sprinkle the chives over the mushrooms and serve.

CRAB WITH MANGO, AVOCADO AND GRATED GINGER

STARTER
SERVES 4

6 oranges
juice of 1 lime
1 tsp Thai fish sauce (nam pla)
2 tsp sesame oil
1 tsp soy sauce
1 ripe mango, peeled and thinly
   sliced

2 ripe avocados, pitted and
   thinly sliced
2 tins of crabmeat (170g/6oz
   each), drained
3cm/1¼in piece of fresh root
   ginger, peeled and grated
cayenne pepper

- Cut some strips of orange zest using a vegetable peeler. Be careful not to peel the white pith as this has a bitter taste.
- Squeeze the oranges and pass the juice through a sieve.
- Put the juice and zest strips in a pan. Bring to the boil, then boil to reduce by half. Make sure the juice doesn't turn brown (colour in the juice indicates caramelisation of the sugars, which you do not want for in this dish).
- Leave the orange juice to cool, then chill in the fridge.
- Take the juice out of the fridge, remove the zest and add a kick of lime juice.
- With a fork, beat in the fish sauce, sesame oil and soy sauce.
- Pour the dressing into four bowls.
- Place the mango, avocado and crab in each bowl.
- Place a tiny dollop of grated ginger on top and sprinkle with cayenne pepper to serve.

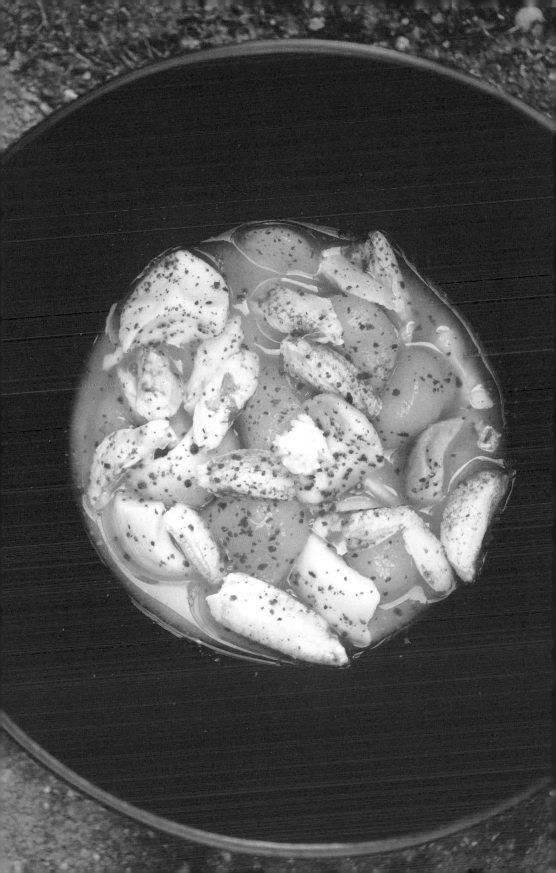

SPECIES	Cockles
BINOMIAL NAME	*Cerastoderma edule*
FISHING METHODS	Cockle hand raking
MSC CERTIFIED	Dee Estuary and Bury Estuary (UK), the Wadden Sea (The Netherlands) (for more information on the MSC see page 152)
TINNED OPTIONS	Cockles in water

A GLASS OF SALTY MANZANILLA MAKES A GOOD ACCOMPANIMENT TO COCKLES.

COCKLES

SPANIARDS love shellfish. You won't find a tapas night without mussels, clams and cockles. These shellfish are in high demand. If fresh shellfish aren't available, they'll happily make do with tinned versions. Tinned cockles are great, because after harvest they're immediately cooked in their own juices and packaged. The cooking liquid is salty and some sandy sediment is not uncommon. A glass of salty manzanilla makes for a good accompaniment to cockles. This sherry from the southern Spanish coast is aged in open storehouses where the sea-salt-heavy Atlantic winds blow freely.

MANY cockles – the *berberechos* – are harvested off the Galician coast in northern Spain, but the catch is not sufficient to supply the high demand. The Spanish have found an ally in the Dutch, who themselves prefer imported *vongole* to their own fleshy cockles from the Wadden Sea. Perhaps a *spaghetti alle cockele* will convince them.

A tin of cockles can be quite pricy, because one tin contains many of these little shellfish, and because of the low demand in the UK, it can be tricky to get hold of tinned cockles. You could purchase them online, or a well-stocked fishmonger will sell them and many Spanish convenience stores will stock tins of *berberechos*. If you're in one of those stores, also get your hands on some fresh chorizo and Spanish rice. These go well with mussels and cockles to make a delicious *arroz*. Add a glass of white wine and enjoy these Spanish delicacies.

RAKING ON THE WADDEN SEA

WITH rhythmic movements, the photogenic Sjors rakes the seabed of the Engelsmanplaat, a sandbank between Ameland and Schiermonnikoog in the Wadden Sea. Sjors is hip-high in the fast-flowing water. A few more scrapes and it's back to the mother ship on a dinghy full of cockles. This raking technique ensures enough cockles are left for the oystercatchers. The fishermen have agreed to leave certain sandbanks in peace and to keep to yearly catch quotas. The MSC-certified cockle fishery in the Wadden Sea is a shining example of fishing while respecting the environment.

COQLADE

MAIN COURSE
SERVES 4

MOUCLADE, mussels in a creamy curry sauce, is a staple in French cuisine from the coastal town of La Rochelle. The French also enjoy their cockles with curry flavours, as in this coqlade.

2 garlic bulbs
250g/9oz chestnut mushrooms
olive oil
2 red onions, chopped
25g/1oz butter
3 onions, finely chopped
3 tsp curry powder
1 glass of dry white wine
100ml/3½fl oz/scant ½ cup
    whipping cream

100ml/3½fl oz/scant ½ cup
    crème fraîche
5 saffron strands
200ml/7fl oz/generous ¾ cup
    chicken stock
sea salt and freshly ground
    black pepper
2 tins of cockles (120g/4¼oz
    each), drained
1 baguette, to serve

- Preheat the oven to 170°C/325°F/gas 3.
- Wrap the bulbs of garlic in kitchen foil. Roast in the oven for 30 minutes until the cloves have softened.
- Clean the mushrooms with a brush and cut into quarters.

- Heat a splash of olive oil in a frying pan. Fry the mushrooms on a medium-high heat until golden brown on all sides.
- Remove the mushrooms from the pan, sprinkle with black pepper and set aside.
- Take the garlic out of the oven and leave to cool.
- Heat the butter in a large, heavy-based pan and fry the finely chopped onions until they're translucent. Add the curry powder and leave to fry for 2 minutes over a low heat.
- Deglaze by pouring in the white wine, and boiling for a minute or so, stirring all the time.
- Cut the top off the bulbs of garlic and squeeze out the cloves. Add the garlic paste to the curried onions.
- Add the cream, crème fraîche and saffron. Leave to simmer very gently for a few minutes. Do not allow the mixture to boil or the crème fraîche may separate.
- Add the chicken stock and a pinch of salt and leave to simmer for a few more minutes.
- Just before serving, add the mushrooms, red onion and cockles.
- Finally add a couple of decent cracks of black pepper and serve with slices of fresh baguette.

COURGETTE AND FENNEL SOUP WITH COCKLES

STARTER
SERVES 4

olive oil
1 baby fennel bulb, chopped
2 courgettes, chopped
5 tbsp chicken stock
a few sprigs of flat-leaf parsley
2 tins of cockles in water
*   (120g/4¼oz each), drained*

sea salt and freshly ground
*   white pepper*
a handful of chives, finely
*   chopped*

- Heat a splash of olive oil in a frying pan over a medium heat. Fry the fennel and courgette for a few minutes, making sure you do not colour the vegetables.
- Add the chicken stock, turn the heat down to low and simmer until the fennel is tender.
- Add a few sprigs of flat-leaf parsley, then purée the soup with a stick blender. You want a chunky consistency.
- Season with salt and pepper.
- Divide the soup among four bowls, then add the cockles to the bowls.
- Drizzle over a little more olive oil and garnish with the chives.

SPECIES	Herring
BINOMIAL NAME	*Clupea harengus*
FISHING METHODS	Pelagic trawl and purse seine
MSC CERTIFIED	Almost all herring from Denmark, The Netherlands and Scotland is certified (for more information on the MSC see page 152)
TINNED OPTIONS	Herring in water, herring with tomato and basil, smoked herring in oil, smoked herring with pepper

HOW ABOUT A TIN OF HERRING WITH TOMATO AND BASIL? THAT'S HOW GOOD TINNED HERRING CAN BE.

HERRING

HERRING is available both plain and smoked, but it is probably smoked herring that is better known, and to many people in the UK, that means kippers, which are available both freshly smoked and in a tin. A Victorian favourite for breakfast and an ingredient in the rice-based, Anglo-Indian dish kedgeree, some people may think of kippers as something quintessentially British. In fact, their popularity has waned considerably over the last century. When it comes to who actually originated kippers, opinions are divided. Conserving food by wood-smoking it is a technique a few thousand years old (if not more). The independent Food and Agriculture Organisation of the United Nations is confident in naming the Dutch as the originators. The old-Dutch word *küppen* was initially used for lean salmon caught outside the season. An interesting kipper is the red herring, a red-brown smoked herring a couple sizes larger than our kipper.

THE UN'S FOOD AND AGRICULTURE ORGANISATION

A real kipper is a split, cold smoked herring. Split lengthways, the filleted fish is connected from head to tail. The Dutch also have the brado, a halved kipper. The origin of brado is undisputed, and the locally famous Ouwehand family takes the credit. In The Netherlands steamed buckling – a hot smoked, steamed herring – is more popular than the kipper. Cold-smoked herring is called a bloater. The buckling and bloater don't end up in a tin, whereas the kipper often does. Tinned kipper is smoked in the same way as 'fresh' kipper. For the tinned variety, the manufacturers can use lean herring, which is also used for pickled herring, rollmops. This herring from the winter months is not fatty enough to be used as soused herring.

MANY manufacturers offer MSC-certified herring, mostly derived from sustainable fisheries in Norway, Denmark or Scotland. These fisheries also fish for soused herring, as does the Dutch vessel, *Hollandse Nieuwe*. They cast out ring nets and close them around a school of herring. The nets don't touch the bottom of the sea, which limits unwanted bycatch. Using this method the fishermen take their responsibility for maintaining healthy fish stocks.

THE major herring processors are found in Denmark and North Germany. Many herring fisheries nowadays meet the requirements set by the MSC. But that's not all. The factories, themselves also MSC-certified, produce delicious tinned fish filled with Scandinavian chefs' cleverly balanced sauces. How about a tin of herring with tomato and basil or a piri-piri-mango sauce? These fish don't need much to go with them – a fresh slice of chunky bread at most. That's how good tinned herring can be.

CULINARY TINNED FISH FROM NORTH GERMANY

FRANK Desler produces good herring in his cannery in the North-German Flensburg with tasty sauces – like tomato and basil – from Scandinavian chefs. He knows everything there is to know about herring and fully supports processing only sustainably caught fish. Preparing his fish, Frank pays close attention to the details. Too much heat can soften the herring too much and Frank does not want herring paste. By parboiling the herring, the fillets soften without losing texture and flavour.

CAULIFLOWER PANNA COTTA WITH KIPPERS

MAIN COURSE
SERVES 4

1 small cauliflower
olive oil
1 leek, white part only, finely chopped
dry white wine
150ml/¼ pint/scant ⅔ cup
   vegetable stock
350ml/12fl oz/1½ cups whipping
   cream
4 leaves of gelatine
1 tin of kippers in oil
   (190g/6¾oz), drained

1 tbsp white wine vinegar
10 capers, finely chopped
1 shallot, finely chopped
2 tbsp olive oil
1 tbsp hazelnut oil
1 tsp chopped flat-leaf parsley
salt and freshly ground white
   pepper

- Cut the cauliflower into large florets, then a quarter into smaller florets.
- Heat a dash of oil in a frying pan and braise the leek on a low heat.
- Add the large cauliflower pieces and cook gently for 10 minutes or so.
- Deglaze with a splash of white wine and leave it to evaporate.
- Add the vegetable stock and season with salt and pepper. Bring to the boil, then leave to simmer gently for about 10 minutes.
- Stir in the cream and leave the broth to settle for 15 minutes. Meanwhile, soak the gelatine leaves in a generous amount of cold water and grease four individual 5cm/2½in ramekins with olive oil.
- When the cauliflower is cooked, purée the mixture, then rub through a sieve. Squeeze the moisture from the gelatine and stir into the mixture until blended. Spoon into the ramekins and chill for about 4 hours.
- Take the panna cottas out of fridge and turn out onto four plates. Arrange the kipper pieces around the panna cotta.
- Beat together the vinegar, capers, shallot and olive oil.
- Heat the hazelnut oil in a frying pan. Fry the smaller cauliflower pieces quickly until lightly browned. Stir through the dressing.
- Pour the dressing over the kippers and garnish with parsley.

KIPPER KEDGEREE

MAIN COURSE
SERVES 4

4 poppadoms
300g/10½oz/1⅔ cups basmati
    rice
100g/3½oz butter
4 tsp curry powder
2cm/¾in piece of fresh root
    ginger, peeled and grated
2 onions, finely chopped
3 tbsp chicken stock
3 eggs, hard-boiled and chopped
5 sprigs of coriander, finely
    chopped

5 sprigs of flat-leaf parsley, finely
    chopped
1 lemon
2 tins of kippers in oil
    (190g/6¾oz each),
    drained
1 bunch of spring onions, cut
    in rings
salt and freshly ground black
    pepper

- Prepare the poppadoms according to the instructions on the packet.
- Cook the rice according to the instructions on the packet. The rice should be al dente, as it will be reheated later. Leave to cool.
- Melt the butter in a frying pan. Add the curry powder and grated ginger and fry for a minute.
- Add the onion and fry until translucent.
- Deglaze with a splash of chicken stock and let the stock evaporate, stirring to mix in all the juices from the pan.
- Add the chopped egg.
- Stir in the rice and heat through over a low heat. Season the kedgeree with the coriander, parsley, a squeeze of lemon juice, salt and pepper.
- Carefully stir the kipper pieces through the kedgeree.
- Serve the kedgeree with broken poppadoms pieces and spring onions.

THIS book was created with the help of many people.

FIRSTLY, I want to thank Harry Visbeen. It's been a joyful and educational experience to cook with you, Harry! I'd also like to thank Franky Visbeen for the copious amounts of work you did in the kitchen. Thanks to Jos Schijff for making the kitchen of the ROC Mondriaan in The Hague available. And thanks to Jaap van Rijn for the wonderful photography.

I'D like to thank all the fishermen who catch the fish that end up in the Fish Tales tins: Zé Manel, Pat Pikus, Ali Mohamed, Poul Kaergaard, Frank Desler, Jack Webster, Mariano Di Scala and Sjors Schonewille.

FOR the welcome and guidance I received in Portugal I thank Maria Cristina, Sofia Brandão, Antonio Cunha, Sergio Real and Joao Coelho at the A Poveira S.A. cannery. For my trip to the Maldives my thanks go to John Burton and the other staff and fisherman at Horizon Fisheries Pvt. Ltd.

I would also like to thank everyone at Kosmos Publishers and especially Melanie Zwartjes who has fully supported this book from the start. Wouter Eertink, thank you for co-ordinating this process and Anne Wouters for co-ordinating the texts. Tijs Koelmeijer, thanks for the beautiful design.

I thank my Fish Tales business partner Harm Jan van Dijk. It's going to be a great venture. Many thanks to Michiel Eliens for being a great help with the photography at Fish Tales. Thanks also to Julie van der Have. Thanks to Leo Hattenbach and Jaap Hoogendijk for believing in Fish Tales.

THANKS to Marcus Polman for his PR and marketing efforts and Judith Renard for the PR at Kosmos Publishers.

I want to thank Ivo van Kempen and everyon at Bagels & Beans, Rogier Soetens and the employees of Bakerstreet, Marc Dotinga and Marco Romeyn at Qizini and Roel Verwiel at KLM.

LAST but not least, my thanks go to my darling Bernadien and my wonderful children Bo and Juul. Lots of love for my friends and family.

BART VAN OLPHEN

NOTES ON THE RECIPES

The drained weight of canned fish is approximate in the recipes. The tablespoons used in this book have a capacity of 15 ml, the dessertspoons of 10 ml, and the teaspoons of 5 ml. Scoops are levelled, unless otherwise indicated.

First published in the UK in 2015 by Pavilion
1 Gower Street, London WC1E 6HD

All rights reserved. No part of this publication may be copied, displayed, extracted, reproduced, utilised, stored in a retrieval system or transmitted in any form or by any means, electronic, mechanical or otherwise, including but not limited to photocopying, recording, or scanning without the prior written permission of the publishers.

ISBN: 978-1-910496-23-7

A CIP catalogue record for this book is available from the British Library.

10 9 8 7 6 5 4 3 2 1

Reproduction by Mission Productions Ltd, Hong Kong
Printed and bound by L.E.G.O. SpA, Italy

Commisioning editor: Emily Preece-Morrison
Translator: Benjamin Broekaert

This book can be ordered direct from the publisher at www.pavilionbooks.com

First published in the Netherlands in 2014 as *Koken Met Vis Uit Blik*
© 2014 Kosmos Uitgevers, onderdeel van VBK|media, Utrecht/Antwerpen
© Text: Bart van Olphen
Concept and recipes: Bart van Olphen
Photography, text and editing recipes: Jaap van Rijn
Editorial Coordination: Anne Wouters
Cover and interior design: Tijs Koelemeijer
Photos page 2, 4 (below), 7, 20, 21 and 27: Bart van Olphen
Photos pages 4 and 75: Chris Arend
Photo page 123: Chris Miller
Photos page 28: Fred Greaves
Photo page 158: Lard Breebaart

SOURCE READING

The French connection in the early history of canning, J. C. Graham, Journal of the Royal Society of Medicine, Volume 74 May 1981
Origins of the Canning Industry, R. A. Bell, The Newcomen Society, 2004

MSC stands for Marine Stewardship Council and is the global standard for sustainable fishing. Only fish and seafood from MSC certified fishery may bear the blue MSC ecolabel. The MSC standard applies three principles: sustainable resources, minimizing environmental impact and effective management. It means that the certified fisheries could continue indefinitely without the resources to be exhausted and the ecosystem is maintained and in compliance with local, national and international laws. For more information about the MSC, see www.msc.org